Table of Contents

In the Beginning
Nanna Byrne
School
Sagging School
Bill Forrester, His Sisters and Me
May Queen
Busking
Nanna Kay
Bath Night
Wash Day
A Packet of Tea
My First Suit
Birkenhead Docks – A History
Dockers' Nicknames
Dockers
High School and Church
What a Waste
The Flat Lanes
The Pine Woods
The Overmantel
Dirty Blue Knickers
Birkenhead Market
The Butcher's Boy
Scouts
Lewis's Ltd.
A History of Lewis's
Lewis's Junior Camp
The Coronation
Mam
The Cocky Rabbit
New Year's Eve 1936
The Chalet

The War Years
Scousers
Joining Up – October 1939
Byrne the Boxer
Windsor Barracks
Wellington Barracks
Guard Duty at Buckingham Palace
Guarding the Railway Bridge
Moving Around
Hats Off
My Pen Friend, Scotland 1941-1942
The Fight with the Cold
A Friend in High Places
Tunisia 1942-1943
Italy
Casino
Back Home
After the War
Moving to Manchester
Passports Please
Father Christmas at Lewis's
The Lewis's Bomb
Security
Sunday Afternoon Trip – December 1997
Ladies Day – 4th June 1998
Golden Wedding – 3rd July 1998
Jim
Tom
Ivy's Story Ivy's words
John's closing notes:
Jacks Eulogy delivered by John

In the Beginning

Dacre Street, Birkenhead

Ah, the first day of Spring—March 21st—a perfectly fine day to be born, if I do say so! It was the year 1920, a year that somehow feels easy to compute in terms of age. Now, however, I find myself wishing I'd arrived in 1930 instead, especially since we're in 1981, and I've just hit the grand old age of 61. I don't feel 61! Sure, I've traded in my squash racket and badminton shuttlecock (I surrendered badminton this year—it was time), but you'll find me on the golf course or sweeping across the dance floor at ballroom dancing. It's all a bit of a 'past-tense' situation now, as I face the looming reality of retirement—just around the corner, in fact. April 1983 can't come fast enough!

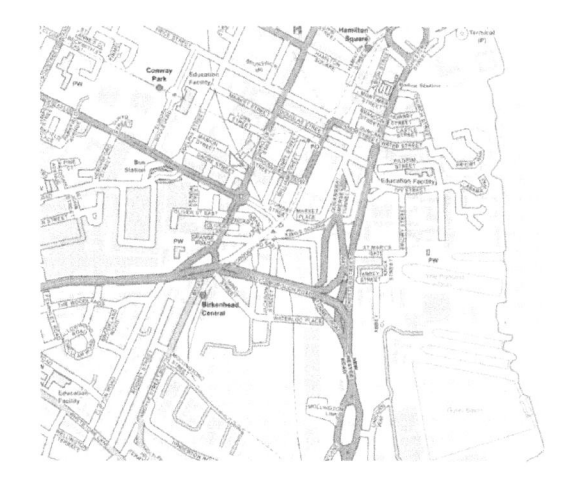

Back in 1920, Dacre Street was all the rage—stylish terraced houses with three bedrooms, a parlour (the posh front room), a kitchen (where the real living happens), and a back-kitchen. Each room was graced with a gas light—except, of course, for the tiny back bedroom, which was probably reserved for the world's quietest guests. The toilet was an adventure in itself, nestled down the yard, and behind it was "the Midden," a brick enclosure where household rubbish went to meet its fate. Picture this: a wooden door, about 2 feet 6 inches square, stationed three feet high, just inviting the adventurous four-year-olds!

Once a fortnight, the "Midden Men"—think of today's refuse collectors in their heroic garb—would scale the Midden wall, shovelling rubbish into wheeled carts like it was an Olympic sport. It took all day! Our little entry, a passageway between two rows of houses, served about a hundred homes, making the day a bit of a community spectacle.

Newspaper article about Dacre Street being demolished

Nanna Byrne

The first four years of my life were largely spent with Nanna Byrne at number 3 Robert Street, and oh, what a time it was! My earliest memories are wrapped in the comfort of her cosy two-bedroom house—popularly known as a "two up, two down." I think I was about four years old when my memories started to form like the layers of an onion.

Nanna was a widow, and I've got a feeling I was her pride and joy. I certainly remembered Grandad Byrne. Why? Because I was his favourite, of course! He'd let me listen to his prized wireless set through headphones. Yeah, we were living large back then! The sound wasn't great—it was like trying to listen to the radio on a tin can—but hey, wireless sets were as rare as hen's teeth! The aerial was a whole production, propped on a pole in the yard and cleverly snaked through the window into the wireless. Quite the engineering feat! Grandad met his unfortunate end at just 59, and while a bit of family lore suggested he "swallowed his tongue," a stroke was to blame in reality.

I can vividly recall his Wake—because let's be honest, being an Irishman meant this was less of a funeral and more of a grand gathering. Grandad lay in his finest suit, collar perfectly starched. As for footwear? Well, knowing him, he was probably sporting boots! The house was small, somewhat like a sardine can, but we managed to fit in over twenty people—mostly men, naturally (at least 90%). The ladies, bless them, handled the sandwiches and the endless pile of mugs. In the kitchen? A barrel of beer sat invitingly, while the ladies opted for the more refined choice of port wine and lemonade.

Everyone who walked in made a beeline for the coffin, offering a kiss and a "Hail Mary." A handful of priests graced us with their presence, but they were hardly the main event! I'm unclear how long the Wake lasted—perhaps two nights? By the third night, Grandad made the trip to St. Laurence's Church, positioned before the High Altar. Friends kept vigil all night, mostly to toast him properly, I suspect. The allure of the barrel kept everyone in good spirits through the night, before the customary Mass at 9:00 a.m., followed by a cemetery visit and, of course, back to Robert Street to finish off the remaining barrel.

Sunday mornings were a treat! After Mass, we'd swing by to see Nanna Byrne at her place, where the spread was nothing short of a feast—bread dipped in hot bacon fat and a hot cup of tea with Carnation milk. Believe me, after fasting since Saturday night, this was a royal banquet! And let's not forget the half penny that Nanna would slip us—which was the highlight of our week! Whether we dashed off to the sweet shop for a sugary delight or made a beeline to the fruit and veg shop for a shiny apple or an orange, Sunday morning felt like a celebratory feast day.

Those simple joys crafted a tapestry of memories that I still hold dear. Each visit with Nanna was filled with warmth, laughter, and love, setting the stage for everything that came after in my adventure of life. Whether it was sharing stories with her about the past or daydreaming about my future, her little two up, two down house was a treasure trove of wisdom and comfort.

Little did I know then, each moment spent with her would become a cherished chapter in my own personal memoir. And as I look back now, I realize these early years were not just a foundation of my childhood; they were the beginning of a grand story waiting to unfold—one filled with characters, joyful moments, and invaluable lessons, seasoned with a sprinkle of humour and a dash of seriousness when life demanded it.

School

My first day at school? Oh, what a whirlwind that was! The vivid memory of those nuns—their black habits and startling white headpieces—still sends shivers down my spine. They were like the 'bogeymen' we were warned about, ready to whisk you away if you misbehaved. But despite that initial fright, I ended up enjoying my time in Infants' School. Each teacher was a character straight out of a storybook, armed with chalk and a generous dose of understanding that made lessons surprisingly enjoyable. At the time, I didn't recognize it, but I actually looked forward to school.

By then, I was the eldest of three or four boys—eventually, our little crew grew to a wild nine boys, with no girls in sight! It might have been the chaos at home that made school feel like a welcome escape. I loved doodling on slates with colored chalk, shaping animals and whimsical figures from clay, and gathering leaves and flowers for collages. Learning to read, write, add, subtract, and multiply was quite the adventure, with plenty of fun along the way.

Alas, my time in the Infants' School was a brief two years, and soon I was off to Junior School. Here, things changed dramatically. Male and female teachers joined the fray, along with a Headmaster who had an infamous reputation—the cane. Yes, that brutal torture device that started with one stroke and somehow escalated to six. I can't recall how we got there, but I'm pretty sure there were several levels in between!

The big boys in Form IV, all the way up to eleven years old, seemed like giants to us. Their size and swagger could be intimidating—they were practically bullies! You quickly learned how to dodge a blow or two, lest you find yourself on the wrong end of a playground scuffle. The headmasters' cane was the ultimate symbol of respect (or fear), and the Priest? Well, he could peer right into your soul, armed with all the knowledge of your sins from confessions past, which somehow made him even scarier.

Sagging School

The first rebellious act I remember took place when I was about seven. There was a boy in my class, nicknamed "Grandad," who was bald from a serious illness. I liked Grandad; we often walked to and from school together since he lived nearby. The older boys were relentless, always tormenting him, but he usually had a remarkable patience that would put a saint to shame.

One fateful day, however, they crossed a line, hurling insults and beginning to physically pick on him. In a fit of anger, I jumped in to defend my buddy, and together we managed to give that ragtag gang a good thrashing. The cry of "Fight, Fight!" rang out, catching the attention of the teacher supervising the playground. Next thing you know, we found ourselves standing before the Headmaster, palms outstretched, as we each received six strokes of the cane for our bravery. Painful? Absolutely. But on the bright side, Grandad wasn't bullied again after that!

Of course, Grandad and I couldn't help but feel the punishment was incredibly unfair, so we decided to sag school for a whole week in protest. As luck would have it, the weather was lovely, and we spent our days lounging on the railway walls, watching the goods trains come and go to Birkenhead Docks and the Abattoir. Those cattle wagons were positively fascinating! I often wonder how long our little rebellion would have lasted if the Headmaster hadn't sent a letter to check on my health. That letter led to an earful from my father and a stern backhander from my mother. Grandad's parents paid a visit to the Headmaster, scolding him for not keeping an eye on those school bullies. Talk about feeling let down—no one seemed to acknowledge my valiant efforts!

Access to our secret hideaway, the railway wall, was through "the field." This place was entirely enclosed, serving as a holding area for telegraph poles—it likely belonged to the GPO. The ten-foot-high fence was quite the fortress! The bottom five feet were reinforced with dug-in railway sleepers, which we used for a little boost to peek over the top. We always kept an arsenal of bricks at the ready to fend off any rival gangs, especially around Bonfire Night when our precious bonfire materials were stashed there. The field actually belonged to the Marion Street Gang, who graciously let our gang join forces, creating an unbeatable alliance against any other street crew.

The field was our "Mecca," a playground of imagination where we spent countless hours building dugouts, trenches, and forts. We played everything from Cowboys and Indians to the brave British soldiers facing off against their German counterparts

We cooked meals and boiled water like we were master chefs, and I remember the day I first learned to smoke out there—not the most pleasant introduction, I must admit. It truly was a boys' world—no girls allowed!

Adjacent to the field was a scrap yard overflowing with old vehicles of every kind: cars, lorries, horse carts, and traction engines. It was like a treasure trove for us! All those metal frames were perfect for constructing our makeshift shelters in the field. Naturally, the yard owners were none too pleased with our passive invasion, keeping two ferocious-looking Alsatians on guard. Their bark could wake the dead, but as far as I remember, nobody ever got bitten. They merely served as an effective deterrent, ensuring we stayed on our side of the fence.

As time passed, however, the field began to lose its allure. A new obsession took hold of us: roller skates! Mr. Whyte, the owner of the corner shop, had an impressive collection. Some skates had ball-bearing wheels—pure luxury! He let us pay a small deposit each week, and once we'd paid half the price, the skates were ours. Before that, if you were unlucky in the skate lottery, you had to beg to borrow a pair from the fortunate kids who'd already hit the jackpot.

Mr. Whyte was also the mastermind behind our grand races around the block. Picture it: Marion Street, Camden Street, Market Street, and down Adelphi Street—all of us zipping past, racing for glory and, of course, a few shouts of envy from onlookers. But beware: one skate could wreak havoc on a pair of shoes really quick!

Just as roller skates hit their peak, push-bikes followed suit. With the scrap yard filled to the brim with bicycle frames and wheels sans tires, we got to work creating makeshift bikes. Some had seats, while others were essentially glorified scooters—you just propelled yourself with your feet! Of course, that resulted in another rapid shoe deterioration.

Ah, the joys of youth! What a wild ride it was, filled with laughter, a few bruises, and endless adventures that carved lasting memories in the tapestry of my childhood. Little did we know how those fleeting moments of freedom and camaraderie shaped us into the men we would eventually become.

Bill Forrester, His Sisters and Me

My very first friend was Bill Forrester—a couple of years younger than me and as sprightly as a spring lamb. I was the eldest in my family, while Bill held the title of the youngest in his crew of siblings, which included five sisters and a brother named Tom. Tragically, Bill's mother had passed away, and his father ran a business dealing in coal, fruit, handcarts—quite the eclectic mix! Back in those days, motorcars were still a novelty, and Bill's dad had a wagon that was the talk of the town, especially when he took us on rides all the way to Moreton Shore. What a treat!

Now, May was the eldest of Bill's sisters, followed by Sarah, Anne, Ivy, and little Eva. Those sisters had distinctly different standards compared to the wild antics we boys thrived on. In my household, you had to fight tooth and nail for everything; it was a classic case of "first up, best dressed." As we grew older, our ragtag gang expanded, transforming our playground into a vast territory stretching from Dacre Street to York Street. Directly across from York Street was Paddy Murphy's shop, and right next door was Bill's house. Poor Bill's sisters had to endure all our racket and chaos—a true test of patience!

We amassed a gang of at least ten boys and four girls (some of whom were the sisters of the boys). As the self-appointed leader, I needed to be tough and possess the loudest voice, thanks in part to my four younger brothers and my very deaf mother! The Forrester girls affectionately dubbed me "Fog Horn," alongside a few less flattering names that I won't repeat. Unfortunately for them, our main activities were centred right outside their house, turning their lives into a perpetual circus!

Inevitably, the girls blamed me whenever something went awry. Take this one time: we were deep into a game of chase when Bill suddenly darted across Conway Street, only to find himself in the path of an oncoming motor car. I bolted to his house, panicking as I relayed the message that Bill had been whisked off to the hospital. May pointed the finger at me, claiming I was to blame for his accident. I hadn't even had the chance to step foot in Conway Street at the time!

Then there was that fateful day when Bill and I decided to help Sarah with the stables, which had become her responsibility after Mr. Forrester passed away. With the horse tethered in the yard, we took a break and engaged in a friendly sparring match inside the stable. When we finally went to bring the horse back in, imagine our horror—he had vanished! We dashed into the street, and a woman called out, "Looking for a horse? It's down Grange Road!" Just our luck! Saturday morning was buzzing with shoppers, mostly women and children because the men were hard at work.

As we sprinted down Grange Road, people pointed and shouted, "The horse is down there!" Our hearts sank as we approached Charing Cross, the busiest junction where five roads converged, and, of course, there was always a Policeman on watch. Just when we thought we'd met our end, we spotted the wayward horse—drinking water from a window cleaner's bucket, of all things! We grabbed the reins and hurried back to the stables, only to be confronted by an irate Sarah.

Before I could explain, she delivered a stunning blow to my ear that left me dazed and confused. Out of the yard I flew, told never to return. It hardly seemed fair—I thought Bill should have been the one taking the hit! But it was clear: I wasn't exactly in the good books with the Forrester girls.

Despite our little escapades, Bill and I remained steadfast friends. When war broke out in 1939, our paths diverged. I was older and would be drafted first, so I decided to enlist and joined the Grenadier Guards, while Bill opted for the Royal Marines. It wasn't until 1946 that we reunited, and he graciously stood by my side as my Best Man. As of 1996, we still keep in touch, often gathering to reminisce about the good old days. With our future planning limited to what we'll have for lunch, we make the most of our time together!

May Queen

Ah, the May Queen processions—what a delightful time to be alive! During the years between 1926 and 1934, those events were all the rage. We boys would wear homemade costumes: Clowns, Pirates,

Cowboys, or Indians, while the May Queen, King, and their entourage of Maids and Page Boys took centre stage. Our role, aside from donning our colourful attire, was to collect money from the generous public as they passed by, both on the streets and in the queues for the cinema. All the proceeds went toward hosting a grand street party that Dacre Street would remember!

Picture this: tables and chairs stretched down the centre of our street, with every mother in the neighbourhood whipping up their finest culinary creations. There were sandwiches, cakes, jelly, blancmange, and delightful fruits served with custard or ice cream. And let's not forget the drinks—bubble-filled lemonade and tangy sarsaparilla overflowing in cups.

Entertainment was provided by our own homemade concert party! A good number of the boys would take to the "stage"—a patch of pavement transformed by our rambunctious energy. Some would sing, others would dance, and George Barzey was a crowd favourite with his guitar, belting out Cowboy songs that struck a chord with everyone. My brother Frank joined in with his renditions of Al Jolson hits, captivating the audience with his enthusiasm. Oddly enough, the girls never seemed to join the singing or dancing—it's not because we didn't want them to, but rather, we never thought to encourage them!

Those May Queen processions brought the whole community together, creating memories filled with joy, laughter, and a sense of belonging that was hard to replicate. It was our way of celebrating spring and the friendships we cherished, crafting connections that, like the delicious jelly and custard, would stick with us for years to come.

As I reminisce about those carefree days—when life was all about friendships, games, and community—it reminds me of how important those moments were in shaping who we've become. From the gang of mischief-makers to the sweet celebrations of the May Queen, those experiences were like it was written in the stars—just another chapter in the story of our lives.

Busking

Every so often, our concert gang would entertain the cinema queue with impromptu performances. While the others sang and danced, my role was to play the money collector and keep an eye out for the Police and rival gangs. One night, in the thick of performance excitement, I spotted my Uncle Jim and Aunt Gladys waiting in line. Feeling cheeky, I handed my collection box to them. Aunt Gladys, with a look of pure disdain, shot back, "Does your mother know you're busking?"

"Yes!" I replied, trying to stand my ground. "I give her the money!" The crowd erupted in laughter, and I couldn't help but feel like a little star. Surprisingly, that night's collection was hefty, but my triumph was short-lived. Aunt Gladys couldn't wait to share the incident with my mother, who didn't find my antics nearly as amusing and gave me a sound thrashing for "showing her up" in front of her friends. At the time, I just couldn't fathom what all the fuss was about!

After that little debacle with Aunt Gladys, we decided to keep our earnings to ourselves. The local Herb-Beer shop was our go-to spot, happily raking in profits with our newfound busking. Balm-Beer or steamy cups of OXO were our favorites depending on the weather, and Kit-Kats or Mars bars were the treats we splurged on. Unfortunately, Ma Baker, the friendly but meddling shop owner, had taken it upon herself to keep my mother informed of our spending habits, thinking we might've been raiding the stash. While that didn't deter our busking, it did put a damper on our visits to her shop!

As we grew older, our spending money didn't increase, and we needed to find new ways to make cash. The busking scene had run its course; our singing and dancing had become old news in the cinema queues. The older, more seasoned buskers even began to threaten us—we were encroaching on their territory!

With my busking days behind me, life took a turn. I had been a Cub Scout and was ready to level up to a Scout. Now that I was old enough, I could also take charge of my younger brothers during the evenings while my mum visited relatives or friends. Our home buzzed with activity, filled with games and laughter from the gang. My evenings were packed with Cubs, the Shaftesbury Boys' Club, trips to the library, and Sunday missions at Thomson's. At this point, girls weren't really on my radar—most of them were just my friends' sisters.

That said, there was one exception: Margaret Francis. She had two brothers in our gang and was a proper tomboy. Not only was she a good sport in our pirate and cowboy games, but she also made an excellent "hostage" for our adventures. We'd tie her up and gag her (all in good fun, of course!). But heaven help you if your hand accidentally wandered where it shouldn't—she was quick to lash out with a wallop that left you knowing you'd crossed a line!

Nanna Kay

The house where we lived actually belonged to my Nanna McKay, or as we affectionately called her, Nanna Kay. Her real last name was Stewart; she had married several times after Grandad McKay passed away. Her last husband, Mr. Stewart, didn't stick around long—he was given his marching orders shortly after the wedding! In total, Nanna had been through three husbands, one of whom was named Dunball. We took great delight in annoying her by singing, "One Ball, Two Ball, Mary Anne Dunball!"

For years, Nanna Kay ran shops, and her last one was a bustling venture in Henry Street near the well-known Rotunda cinema. It was a general store, selling everything from sweets and tinned goods to tobacco, but what drew in the crowd was her incredible baking and cooked food, especially on Friday and Saturday nights. I was her trusty assistant, working as the porter and cleaner on those busy evenings. Locals would frequent the pubs on those nights and send their eldest children to "Nanna Kay's" around 10:00 p.m. to fill their orders.

Oh, the sight of all those pots and pans lugged in was something to behold! Pig's cheek and cabbage was the all-time favourite (though the locals cheekily referred to it as "Pig's Arse and Cabbage"!).

Nanna Kay lived above her shop in Henry Street, but she had a rather unusual companion—a giant male goose that was more effective than a guard dog in her eyes. Let me tell you, that creature scared the daylights out of me! With its neck stretched out, wings flared wide, and an ominous hissing sound that could send chills down your spine, I always felt a profound sense of relief when my work day ended at 11:30 p.m.

After clocking out, I'd hustle to catch a tram to the Pier Head and then hop on the midnight ferry to Woodside, racing home with my heart still pounding from the goose encounters. My mother would usually be waiting for me, and she'd always offer me a comforting cup of tea. Ah, tea! I would have loved to indulge, but as I would be taking Holy Communion at Sunday Mass, I couldn't "break my fast" after midnight.

Nanna Kay was quite the character—a tall, striking woman with flowing black hair, always dressed in a high-necked black lace dress adorned with a pearl necklace or brooch. She had this regal presence about her, even if she was known for having a vicious tongue that could cut like a knife.

When Nanna Kay would come to stay with us, it was like inviting chaos into our home. Her dynamic with my dad resembled a game of tug-of-war—think of a stray cat and an irritable dog forced to coexist under the same roof. It was always entertaining to witness, albeit a bit tense!

Eventually, Nanna sold her shop in Liverpool and bought a smaller one in Hind Street, not far from the Gas Works. This new venture was primarily a sweets and cigarette shop. But the best part? She lived right above the shop—"Thank God for that!" I would often think, glad to be spared another goose encounter when she wasn't around to keep watch.

Reflecting back on those days spent in Nanna Kay's company, I chuckle at the vibrant tapestry of life woven through her various marriages, her bustling shop, and the peculiarities that came with it all. Each little incident, each slice of life from that era, contributed to a collection of stories that envelop my childhood and shaped who I became.

It seemed that every moment was a new adventure worth sharing, from busking and performing to late-night ferry rides and the fascinating quirks of family life. And through it all, the love and laughter of family remained a constant backdrop, grounding me through the chaos of it all.

Bath Night

Despite the myriad challenges of being a large family, particularly with our regular work being scarce, we were exceptionally well cared for, all thanks to Mam. It's only in the years since her passing that we've truly come to appreciate the fierce loyalty and tireless effort she dedicated to keeping her family together. Honestly, managing nine boys must have been a Herculean task that would tire out even the most resilient soul!

Every Friday night was designated bath night at 64 Dacre Street, and let me tell you, it was a colossal undertaking! In our back kitchen stood a massive brick-built boiler that was more of a dinosaur than an appliance. The night would kick off with the daunting task of lighting the boiler—no small feat! Once the flames were roaring, we'd fill the boiler with cold water, of which there were no hot water tanks in sight. Picture this: we'd haul buckets from the tap to the boiler—a full hour's job!

Once the water was approaching boiling, it was time for the laborious process of ladling hot water into the galvanized bath, set up right in front of the fireplace in the dining room. I, as the eldest, bore the weighty responsibility of overseeing "the order of the bath." After three of my younger brothers had their turns, it was back to square one—changing the water, which was another time-consuming affair.

We always used Lifebuoy soap, which lathered brilliantly but had a knack for finding its way into your eyes, no matter how tightly you squeezed them shut. The sting was unbearable, but it didn't hold a candle to Mam's infamous "soft scrubbing brush" routine! After enduring that purgatory and finally getting cleaned up, a cozy hot drink and a biscuit were my small rewards before heading off to bed, freshly scrubbed and ready for Church the next morning. For some of us who had taken our first Holy Communion, that meant no eating or drinking until after the service.

As I grew older, I discovered the luxuries of the public baths in Argyle Street. Oh, what a treat it was to have a bath all to myself!

Recently, during a visit to Birkenhead, I thought I'd take a stroll down memory lane and check out The Baths and our old home at 64 Dacre Street. To my shock, the entire area had undergone a transformation. Everything had been razed and rebuilt, with only Conway Street School still holding some semblance of familiarity. Time certainly marches on, doesn't it?

Wash Day

Now, let me tell you about the normal routine of keeping our home in order—keeping it clean and tidy was not something we ever gave much thought to. Take wash day, for instance; Mam would be up bright and early at 6:30 a.m. But here's the kicker: "wash day" was a misnomer! It actually kicked off on Monday morning and stretched all the way into late Wednesday!

Her first mission? Get the boiler hot, then tackle the first load of washing, which was always the heavy stuff. The real back-breaker, though, was feeding those clothes through the wringing machine in the back yard. And let me tell you, wintertime was a nightmare for this task! It was utterly hellish to be outside in the dark during those chilly mornings. Some days, the weather was "brass monkey" cold!

Inside, we had a clothes-drying rack in the living room, a pulley system with four bars that, when fully loaded, looked like a scene straight out of a Chinese laundry. From Monday night through Wednesday evening, Mam would spend her time ironing those heaps of clothes—a monumental job for one woman, especially with no electric irons to lend a hand. We had two trusty flat-irons which we heated up on the gas stove. No ironing boards for us; we ironed right on the dining table! To test the heat of the iron, you'd spit on the plate, and if the spit sizzled, you were good to go.

Mam's daily routine kicked off at 6:30 a.m. with the fire being raked out (prepped the night before, naturally), followed by Dad's breakfast, and then she'd change and feed the latest baby in the line-up—there was always a baby! By the time we lumbered downstairs around 8 o'clock, we faced the dreaded task of washing up—a rude awakening involving freezing cold water from the sink in the back kitchen. Breakfast was typically porridge made with water (Milk? What's that?!), along with a round of toast and a cup of tea. After that, it was off to school for us!

School became our primary occupation, with Saturday and Sunday reserved for playtime. And oh, how Mam fretted over our shoes! She often patched up with cardboard, especially when holes developed—definitely not a pleasant experience, particularly in wet weather! It was a constant struggle to keep us boys looking presentable, especially given the beat-up state of our footwear.

Still, amidst all the chaos, there was a rhythm to our lives—an unspoken understanding of how crucial each of us was to the household. Mam was the heartbeat of our family, ensuring everything ran smoothly, even if it meant sacrificing her own comfort. As the eldest, I could sense the weight of responsibility slowly shifting onto my shoulders; I felt like I was stepping into her shoes, learning to keep an eye on my younger brothers and assist Mam wherever I could.

Wash days and bath nights were not just chore days; they became a part of our family's culture. Each Friday night bath was like a rite of passage, a moment when, after all that scrubbing and suffering, we emerged clean and fresh, ready to face the world on Sunday. And on wash days, I witnessed the resilience and determination of my mother, driving home the idea that hard work was the cornerstone of family life.

Those moments around the dining table, where we'd make do with limited space while ironing, were our quiet times together—a chance for us to bond over some minor chaos, swapping stories and having a laugh or two.

Looking back, it's incredible how these seemingly mundane routines formed the backbone of my childhood. They instilled in me the importance of family, the value of hard work, and the idea that even the most challenging days could be met with resilience and humour.

Now, as I reminisce, I take comfort in knowing that those laundry days and Friday night baths were not just chores; they were the fabric of our family life, stitching us together in a community built on love, laughter, and the occasional scuffle over a bar of Lifebuoy soap.

In that little home at 64 Dacre Street, we were more than just nine boys under one roof; we were a resilient crew led by the unwavering spirit of Mam, bound together by the shared memories of laughter and life's little trials.

A Packet of Tea

I was just nine years old, and as the leader of our gang, it was my responsibility to keep our activities organized. Saturday mornings were always a bit tricky until Alfie Brown's henhouse became available. With a little tidying up, it turned into the perfect spot for our gang meetings.

Most Saturdays, after our meeting, the real excitement awaited us at the Queen's Hall Cinema, our beloved Mecca. Picture this: each Saturday featured a new episode of a serial. We had to keep up to make sure our hero wouldn't meet a grim fate—typically portrayed in the nail-biting closing moments. You could always count on a train barrelling towards him or a stampede of wild animals ready to trample him flat. Since the films were silent, the audience became part of the entertainment with their howls and shouts of warning, creating a buzz that was electricity in the room. Talking films were just starting to make the rounds, but sadly, they hadn't made it to our beloved cinema yet.

On this particular Saturday, we gathered in Alfie's shed at 10:00 a.m. for our weekly meeting. One of us always had to bring tea-making supplies, and this time it was my turn. With my mother in the hospital getting ready to welcome my fifth brother, Dad was off at work, and Nanna Kay was shopping. I snatched a packet of tea and some biscuits from the shelf and headed to the shed.

The meeting went smoothly, and just as I wrapped things up, I headed home for dinner. But as I approached our house, I could hear an absolute ruckus—like an army engaged in a full-blown battle! It was impossible to tell who was making the most noise, my Nanna or Dad—they were both going at it.

I stepped inside, hoping my presence would help ease the tension, but Nanna's voice rang out: "I've been accused of stealing a packet of tea!" Dad fired back, "There was a packet of tea on the shelf when I left, and now it's gone!"

In a moment of impulsivity, I blurted out, "I took the tea off the shelf!" Both Nanna and Dad turned to me, disbelief etched on their faces, as I pulled the half-full packet from my pocket and placed it on the table. That was the last straw for Dad. Without a word, he swung at me, landing a stunning blow to my head, and then he removed his belt, lashing out in a blind rage. By the time he was done, I was a mess—my shirt ripped, my back lacerated, and Nanna was screaming that she'd report him for cruelty.

I stumbled up the stairs to my room, hardly able to put one foot in front of the other. Somehow, I made it to bed. My back throbbed, and the pain was unbearable. Nanna, clearly furious with Dad, took care of me, seething with anger and plotting her revenge. I managed to calm her down by pointing out the reality: if Dad got jail time, we would be much worse off. She eventually cooled down, but it was obvious that tensions weren't over.

For a week, I stayed in bed, nursing my wounds while Mam returned home with the new baby. The fresh arrival shifted the focus away from my bruises, and although my back felt tender, the pain was bearable compared to the emotional chaos of that day. Everyone in the street caught wind of my plight—Nanna made sure of that! When I went back to school the following week, my teacher commented on how well I looked, saying, "The attack of the flu has done you some good." Little did he know the truth behind my absence!

Looking back, these physical punishments from my Dad left a lasting imprint on us all. To my knowledge, not one of my brothers resorted to violence to discipline his kids. In fact, I've never raised a hand to either of my two boys in anger; instead, they faced threats, had their privileges stripped away, and were made to apologize when they misbehaved. There was a cane perched on the top shelf in the kitchen, used solely as a threat—but it was enough to keep us in line.

As a child, I discovered early on that making a loud fuss during punishment was an effective strategy. I'd wail and sob, ensuring Mam felt she'd had an impact. But come bedtime? One cup of tea and a biscuit always magically found their way to me, and I'd be out in the street, back with my gang, ready to forget everything. Mam often saw through our antics, though. She knew exactly when we were trying to pull the wool over her eyes and made a point to deliver her own form of discipline

My First Suit

I must have been about ten years old when I wore a suit for the first time, and boy, did it feel special! I started my day with 9:00 a.m. Mass, then made a pit stop at Nanna Byrne's before gathering my gang of four to head off to the Thermopylae Pass. The Pass, nestled next to Bidston Hill, was steep and rocky, filled with towering trees that provided plenty of sturdy branches. In hindsight, I probably should have gone home to change out of my suit, but the allure of the great outdoors and our favourite game of tracking was too strong to resist.

This time, I was the designated "escaped prisoner." I was given a head start to leave clues and markings indicating my direction, and my plan was simple: I'd circle around, climb up a tree, and watch the gang search for me. Once my time limit was up, I'd drop down to reveal my hiding spot.

As I descended through the branches, disaster struck: I felt a tear on my sleeve. There was no need to mention the trouble I'd face when the gang discovered it. Thankfully, George Barzey chimed in, suggesting that his mother might be able to fix the tear. If anyone could mend my suit, it was Mrs. Barzey! We hurried back home, and she worked her magic, performing a wonderful patch job. However, there was a noticeable spot where the fabric had caught in the tree.

That's when George had a brilliant idea—instead of worrying about the patch, we could cover it with soot! We went ahead and did just that; surprisingly, it worked like a charm!

Weeks later, however, my mother noticed the tear. I quickly spilled the entire story, and she assured me she wouldn't tell Dad. I was relieved because I knew Dad would react with his belt, which would leave me out of commission for a week! Just as I was revelling in my good fortune, tragedy struck: a well-timed right cross from Mam knocked me across the room. Before I could regain my balance, another quick blow caught me on the other side. It felt like I had been hit by a tornado—the blows came so fast and furious that I was lucky to still be standing! At that moment, I couldn't help but think maybe Dad's belt would have been a gentler punishment!

It wasn't a secret to anyone on the street that Mam was furious about the damage to my suit. Of course, "new" was a relative term by then, but Mam didn't take kindly to any form of fooling around! Once she'd dealt her punishment, she marched over to Mrs. Barzey, who was quite petite and reserved. Knowing that news of her discovery had reached Mam, Mrs. Barzey braced for impact. Instead of a confrontation, though, Mam congratulated her on the fantastic sewing job! Having vented her frustrations, my mother felt satisfied, and all was well that ended well.

I quickly recovered from my thrashing, but it was at least three years before I got another new suit. Mam had her own unique way of disciplinary action—not out of anger but rather as a means to teach a lesson, and she was always effective!

23

Birkenhead Docks – A History

1801: Birkenhead has a population of just 100.

1824: The Iron Works open in Birkenhead North (Wallasey Pool).

1840: The population reaches 8,200, and the railway to Chester is opened.

1843: Birkenhead Docks are built by William Laird.

1858: The Iron Works grow too small and move to Tranmere Pool (Lairds).

1861: The population soars to 61,000, with 62 percent being migrants from Ireland, Scotland, and Wales.

1862: This marks the peak of Irish immigration. By 1911, many Irish were second-generation and predominantly Catholic, with dock work being the primary employment avenue for these migrants.

1871: The population stands at 65,000, with 6,408 houses—78 of which are empty. Many unemployed families looked after one another, fostering a family tradition centred around dock work.

1886: The Mersey Railway is inaugurated, featuring a tunnel running beneath St. Laurence's Church, which eventually had to be torn down due to safety concerns.

1887: Significant shipping lines operating from Birkenhead Docks include Blue Funnel Line, Anchor Line, City Line, Hall Line, Rathbone Line, Pacific Line, and the Clan Line, among others.

Despite the bustling activity, the docks were not without their challenges. There were many strikes throughout the years—far too many for the workers' liking. Pay was meagre, and working conditions were often poor and dangerous. However, there was a steady stream of men seeking work, knowing full well the tough life ahead. Slowly but surely, conditions began to improve as unions gained acceptance, leading to better wages and safer workplaces.

During the war years, the docks played a crucial role, performing admirably in support of the war effort. Yet, in the aftermath, the Mersey Docks faced a decline in trade for various reasons, with the lingering effects of numerous strikes playing a key role in this downturn.

The majority of dock workers were Catholic, and they tended to live in the same neighbourhoods and socialize in the same pubs, making it relatively easy to organize strikes. In contrast, the Liverpool docks—stretching nine miles long—were more fragmented, complicating efforts to hold meetings and rallies within their workforce. Moreover, Birkenhead had its own challenges, including tensions with the Protestant population, particularly members of the "Orange Lodge," who were more prevalent in Liverpool. The dockers harboured a deep-seated mistrust of the shipping fleet owners, considering them thieves and dishonest brokers.

The reality for many in the dock labour force was tough; they were their own worst enemies, often caught in an intricate web of economic necessity, community identity, and intergroup rivalry. Over time, the struggles and victories within Birkenhead's docks painted a rich tapestry of the industrial history that shaped not just the landscape but the very fabric of its community.

As I reflect on this history, I see echoes of my family's struggles and resilience mirrored in the stories of the dock workers. Just as I learned life lessons through my experiences at home, the dockers faced their own trials that forged a strong community bond among them—one that would influence subsequent generations as they navigated the ever-changing tides of work, family, and ambition.

Dockers' Nicknames

In the bustling atmosphere of the docks, nicknames became a necessity. With some families boasting five or more relatives aboard the same ship—Byrnes, Murphys, Kellys, Cavanaghs, Quinlans, and others—these monikers helped distinguish one worker from another. Here are some of the more colourful nicknames that echoed through the docks:

- **"Handbag"**: A bit of a joke, as he was often carried by his mates.
- **"Dodger"**: When he wasn't picked for work, he'd dodge along the line hoping to get chosen later.
- **"Ducky"**: Had flat feet and walked in a way that resembled a duck.
- **"Spitting Mick"**: When he talked, he'd shower you with spit—definitely the life of the party!
- **"Whingin' Mick"**: Always found fault in everything around him.
- **"Blind Jim"**: With a squint that left him nearly blind, he didn't see much at all.
- **"Speccy Byrne"**: His spectacles? Bought from none other than Woolworths.
- **"The Three Wise Men"**: Tommy, Matty, and Joey—blessed with empty heads and plenty of mischief.
- **"Rigger Byrne"**: Quite a character, he had six stitches on one side of his head and eight on the other. After a pint at lunchtime, he was off home!
- **"Putty Nose"**: Had his nose broken but couldn't recall who had done the deed.
- **"Slipaway Sam"**: Always slipping off somewhere, never quite where you expected him to be.
- **"Broken Boomerang"**: A quirky fellow who never seemed to come back.
- **"Seldom Seen"**: He was rarely seen working, but you could count on his presence at the pub!

- **"The Sleeping Solicitor"**: Somehow always asleep on the job.
- **"The Weight Lifter"**: He was the one who waited while you did all the heavy lifting.
- **"The Gunslinger"**: He was notorious for shooting off an hour early.
- **"The Man in Black"**: Always on his way to a funeral—hardly a day passed without hearing about his latest departure.
- **"The Lemon Drop Kid"**: He was known for his sharp wits; you could never make a sucker out of him!
- **"Steam Roller"**: If there was a showdown, he'd flatten you in no time.
- **"High Noon"**: He was always knocked off an hour before noon.
- **"Friday Fred"**: The man never showed up on Fridays, preferring the comforts of the pub.
- **"Steamfly Kelly"**: His whereabouts were usually in the galley, indulging in snacks.
- **"The Vicar"**: With his booming, "Hey, men, hey men!" he could be heard from miles away.
- **"The President"**: Always found at The Whitehouse pub.
- **"The Horseman"**: A legendary figure, loaded six horse boxes but somehow only found five horses—nobody knew what happened to the sixth!

The humour among the dockers was palpable, full of camaraderie and wit. But as time marched on, the humour seemed to fade from the present dockers. The job has shifted dramatically, with most work now centred around containers. Everything is packed into containers at factories beforehand, and even the ships themselves have been designed to accommodate these new methods of operation.

One popular pastime among the dockers was whippet racing. The races were held on a track located in Gorsey Lane, and one whippet that stood out was owned by Grandfather Byrne. His beloved racing dog was whimsically named "Mick the Miller," a nod to the famous greyhound, but he was just a humble whippet enjoying the thrill of the chase!

Dockers

I was about eleven years old when the reality of our financial situation truly hit me. My father worked as a dock labourer, but he was out of work more often than he was in. The system used to select laborers was known as "The Stand." Dockers would line up, waiting for "The Ganger" (the foreman) to walk down the line and pick the men he needed for the day. Each gang consisted of eighteen men, typically assigned to work just one hatch, and most ships boasted five hatches.

Unfortunately, the Gangers often favored their friends and relatives when choosing workers. This system left many men—like my dad— without work for long stretches. If he had a bad week with no jobs, there was no "Dole" (unemployment benefits) to fall back on. If you

28

didn't work, you didn't earn, and that meant turning to The Parish for assistance. Even if it was just a pound, it was something, and any bit helped. The Gangers' selective practices were greatly resented by the dockers, leading to frequent strikes; interestingly, it was the onset of World War II that ultimately prevented any serious showdowns from escalating.

Back in 1921, dockers earned 16 shillings per day, but by 1923, that pay had plummeted to just 10 shillings. The workdays typically stretched from 8:00 a.m. until 12:00 noon, followed by a break for lunch until 1:00 p.m., then back at it until 5:00 p.m. Overtime was always welcome, but there was no set end time—if a ship was due to sail, the work continued until everything was completed.

Before the formation of "The Dock Union," the situation was dire; as many as 4,000 men could be languishing "On the Stand" for just a single ship. Over time, dockers began to align into groups working for specific shipping lines. This system often forced dockers to work only two days and then claim "Public Assistance," as working three days or more disqualified them from that support. There was no shelter from the elements, no canteens, and everything was just tough and rough.

Despite the inconsistent income, my father always seemed to have enough money for a night out drinking. I couldn't recall a time when he took my mother out; it seemed logical at first given we had three or four young children to care for. But he eventually got used to going out alone. My mother, who was quite deaf, relied on lip reading and developed a loud voice. However, that didn't quite fly in a pub atmosphere.

While my father spent time at the pub, my mother often went to the cinema at least twice a week. The Saturday matinee usually lasted from 2:00 p.m. until 4:30 or 5:00 p.m. When Dad returned home from his drinking excursions, he'd typically be in a foul mood. We children would be tucked in bed, but it was impossible to miss the noise that erupted once he came through the door.

My mother had her ways of dealing with any potential aggression. She would heat up the poker in the fire until it was glowing white hot. If Dad ever made any threatening move toward her, out would come the poker, and he didn't stick around to stick around for that. As a result, my mum would sleep on the sofa downstairs, and come morning, all would often be forgotten—like a bad dream brushed aside.

High School and Church

At the age of eleven, it was time to leave St. Lawrence's RC Primary School behind and embark on a new journey at St. Hugh's Central School. I had the opportunity to attend Grammar School, but the reality was that we simply couldn't afford the uniform, let alone the myriad other expenses that came with it. So, off I went to St. Hugh's, where I found myself in the top form for my age—Form 2F, with the "F" signifying our studies in French.

Every Saturday, I dutifully attended Confession, repeating the same sins week after week. I thought I was being clever by choosing a different priest each time, but years later, Father Goodier let me in on a little secret: he knew exactly what I was up to. When I mentioned Canon Baines, he chuckled and remarked that Canon Baines put the fear of God into the priests just as much!

Sunday Mass was a regular fixture in our lives, and we received Holy Communion weekly, except for those occasions when the holes in our shoes were simply too glaring to ignore. Religion was woven into the fabric of every school. While there were many religious denominations, the predominant ones in our area were Roman Catholic and Church of England. Among our gang, there were only two Catholic families: the Byrnes (us) and the Hurleys. We attended the 9:00 a.m. Mass, while the rest of our gang would either go to Sunday School or the Evening Service.

I truly believe our religious upbringing and active participation in church and Scouts helped keep us on the straight and narrow. Every Friday evening, a priest would visit our house, and we all made a concerted effort to be out when he called—there was always a chance that it might be the priest who was also my Father Confessor!

Looking back at the parental advice we received, it's remarkable that we survived at all. The pitfalls were ever-present, and any inquiry about life was usually met with one of the usual responses: "At your age, you ought to know better," or "How many times must I tell you?" Often followed by, "Don't be stupid," or "I've sweated my fingers to the bone trying to raise you properly, and what thanks do I get?" These outbursts were typically shouted loud enough for our friends to hear, adding insult to injury.

Such tirades would often end with a swift blow—if you ducked under the first one, you'd generally find yourself caught by the backhand. It taught us to think twice before asking questions. The concept of parents engaging in conversations about life didn't exist for us; Child Psychology was a notion yet to be discovered. I had no idea that my father's belt could serve purposes other than inflicting pain. Knowing how much it hurt certainly served as the ultimate deterrent.

Another strategy employed to keep us in line was the tale of mythical children—the perfect ones who never misbehaved, who were polite, tidy, and a credit to their parents. Unlike us, with our unruly ways! I swore to myself that if I ever crossed paths with one of those children, I'd give them a good thrashing for being such goody two-shoes!

What a Waste

During the years between 1920 and 1940, our holidays consisted of school breaks and the occasional celebration like Christmas and Easter. Family holidays were a luxury reserved for the wealthy. Sometimes, Mam would take us for a sail on the ferry across the Mersey to Liverpool, or we'd arrange a day trip to the beach at Egremont, nestled halfway between Seacombe and New Brighton. There, we'd find sand, sea, and the pier—a perfect spot for a day out. We often gathered with three or four mothers and their children, along with a few extra kids from the neighbourhood whose mothers could not join us.

As children, our favourite pastime by the sea was crab fishing, whether scouring the rocks or trying our luck under the pier. That pier was always bustling with activity; it was the popular spot for crab hunting. To catch these little crustaceans, all you needed was a piece of string and a cockle or a piece of fish. We'd haul in crabs of all sizes, which we would bring home and toss into a zinc bath filled with saltwater. Sadly, within days, all the crabs would be dead, and Mam would be furious. Not only had we used up all her salt, but she had also predicted their inevitable demise, proclaiming it plain murder.

On one particular outing, we had been fishing for some time when the tide turned, becoming quite rough. I was rounding up our gang when I suddenly heard a loud scream, followed by a chorus of shouts and panic. A girl had been swept off the rocks by the incoming tide. I watched as a man dove in from above, while a nearby boat full of children circled around her. The boat's owner also jumped into the churning water, reached the girl, and handed her safely to the men in the boat.

Everyone's attention was glued to the girl and the rescue efforts, and in the shuffle, no one seemed to notice that the man who had dived in was now missing. Other boats began to arrive, transporting the girl to the beach, where a policeman was pumping water from her. An ambulance came, whisking her away to the hospital. But soon enough, the focus shifted back to the man who had jumped in to save her. Several men entered the water, diving down to search for the missing hero, but despite their efforts, he was nowhere to be found.

Mam hurried us home, and everywhere we looked, mothers were crying. The promenade overflowed with people walking solemnly in the same direction. It felt as though we were part of a funeral procession, a collective mourning for the loss that had occurred that day.

Fast forward ten years, I found myself visiting my cousin, and he took me to meet a friend. We were talking at the friend's front door when we heard a dreadful commotion coming from inside—his sister was having a loud argument with their mother. The quarrel stemmed from this young lady being heavily made up and insisting she was heading to the Woodside Hotel to meet her friends from the ships. It was common knowledge that men from the ships tended to have one-track minds.

As Charles and I walked away, he casually mentioned that the sister of his friend was none other than the girl who had been saved from drowning all those years ago. The man who had heroically jumped in to save her had tragically drowned in the process. He was a married man with five children. It was said that the weight of the copper in his pockets, along with his oilskin trousers filling with water, dragged him down to his fate. A fund was organized to support his family, and it received generous backing from the community. Yet, reflecting on the tragedy, it felt like such a waste—a good man had lost his life for the sake of that young lady.

The Flat Lanes

Today, Brooklands Cricket Club sits at the end of my back garden. Just last weekend, I took a stroll around the edge of the ground, and my mind wandered back to Oxton Cricket Club, nestled on the outskirts of Birkenhead, and to the entrance of the "Flat Lanes," as I fondly remember them. The reason for these memories resurfacing was simple: Brooklands was facing off against Oxton that day in a much-anticipated cricket match.

In the 1930s, our school holidays stretched over five glorious weeks. We spent the last week of July and the first four weeks of August exploring the local parks, the Arno, Seacombe shore, the Flat Lanes, and Bidston Hill—each location offering its unique charm. The Flat Lanes had everything a young boy could wish for: miles of picturesque countryside, a large pond teeming with Jacksharpes, askers, frogs, and even frogspawn. The busy railway nearby added to the excitement, with train drivers often tossing lumps of coal for fuel, which made for lively distractions. Meanwhile, the farmers' fields provided a bounty of potatoes, carrots, swedes, and cabbages, ripe for the picking!

On the Oxton side, magnificent houses with sprawling orchards caught our attention—until, that is, some of our gang found themselves caught raiding the fruit trees. Fortunately, the owner opted not to involve the police; instead, he accepted a promise from us not to pilfer any more fruit. Ironically, it turned out to be the girls who got nabbed, despite being there to keep an eye on the younger children in our crew.

At 5:00 p.m., the girls would escort the little ones home, leaving three or four of us behind to set up a makeshift tent for the night. If the weather turned sour, we would migrate into the railway tunnel. That tunnel was a cold and eerie spot, and we'd find ourselves praying for dawn to break. More often than not, we would be home well before our parents had even risen; my mother always woke up by 7:00 a.m. Looking back, we claimed to enjoy our nights camping out, but the comfort of our own beds was always a welcome relief.

The only place where the girls drew the line was "The Haunted House." Far larger than an ordinary home, it stood on Gorsey Lane as a charred wreck. The floors had collapsed, and crossing from one side to the other required careful navigation along the exposed girders. The smell was unbearable, the darkness oppressive, and there was nothing to entice us to linger apart from the thrill of its haunting reputation, which effectively kept the girls at bay.

Nearby, a fantastic fishing pool added to our adventures, but I imagine that whole area is fully developed now, bereft of the haunted house, the fishing pool, and the excitement that those childhood holidays used to bring.

The Pine Woods

Most of the time, we organized our own entertainment. Being responsible older siblings, we had to take our younger brothers and sisters along, which meant we often welcomed the older girls into our group. They were a valuable addition, watching over the little ones while we immersed ourselves in our games. Our favourites included tracking or chasing each other around the area—whether it was Bidston Hall, the pine woods, or the park—those were happy days! Fishing for Jacksharpes also offered us plenty of excitement.

Birkenhead Park, the first public park in England, was a popular destination for us. It had everything we needed, but we were often annoyed by "Daddy Quick," the park policeman. He was notorious for blowing his whistle constantly, which we kids were sure was aimed at us! Years later, when he retired, he shared a light hearted anecdote about his methods; he'd simply cycle around, blow his whistle, and watch as all the children scattered, thinking he was after them.

While I often mentioned how the girls helped us, we didn't consider that we were providing them with protection in return. One particular day, we set up camp in the heart of the pine woods, an open area devoid of trees, with the toilets conveniently nearby. As we engaged in our customary game of 'Fox and Hounds,' a sudden commotion erupted. Screams and shouting filled the air, causing utter chaos. We hurried back to our headquarters to find some of the girls were crying, and a crowd had gathered outside the toilets.

Soon, two people emerged from the men's restroom, escorting a young man of about twenty years old. It took quite a bit of coaxing to get an explanation out of our girls; each one seemed to have a different version of what had unfolded. Eventually, we learned that this man had attacked one of the girls. She had fought back fiercely, reportedly biting his finger—some claimed she had even bitten it off! There were older women among the crowd who, in a fit of indignation, suggested that she should have targeted something more private!

When the girl finally emerged from the toilets, I was honestly baffled—no man in his right mind would want to associate with someone who looked so dishevelled and unkempt. The young man insisted that the girl had attacked him first, and he was merely defending himself, but the women were having none of it; they were ready to string him up!

Though we were too young to fully grasp the situation, we learned later that our presence had somehow helped protect the girls from what could have been a terrible fate. When we returned home, and each girl relayed the incident to their mothers, the consensus was that we, as boys, had provided invaluable safety on that day.

In the days that followed, we heard whispers that the girl involved had a reputation for creating scenes like the one we had witnessed that day. She was eventually taken to the hospital, but after that, we never heard anything more about her. One thing was certain: the girls never joined us at the pine woods again

The Overmantel

Our house on Dacre Street had six rooms—three living rooms and three bedrooms. The front room downstairs was known as the Parlour, and it housed some furniture that had belonged to Nanna Kay, including a gorgeous sideboard. Atop that sideboard sat an elegant overmantel, adorned with six small shelves supported by delicate columns of cut glass. The top was crafted from finely shaped walnut wood, and at its centre was a large mirror that added to its beauty.

One Friday night, with Mam, Dad, and Nanna all out, I had my gang over, and we decided to play cards. The cards were on top of the overmantel, so I had to precariously stand on the arm of a wooden rocking chair to reach them. Just as I was grabbing the cards, the rocking chair shifted beneath me. I lost my balance, reached for the overmantel, and in a disastrous moment, the whole lot came crashing down! The thunderous noise echoed through the room, and I found myself surrounded by shattered glass and Nanna's cherished trinkets. What could I possibly say to Nanna about this?

Just then, our cat, Buller, sauntered into the room and headed straight for a parcel containing some boiled ham that Mam had intended for sandwiches. In a moment of desperation, I decided to tell the gang to get out and asked Tom Francis if we could go to his house instead. Thankfully, his parents were at the cinema, and his sister agreed to let us hang out there. Once everyone had cleared out, I tidied up the mess as best I could, locked Buller in the parlour, while he enjoyed the ham, and made my way to the Francis's house.

When Nanna returned and discovered Buller in the parlour amidst the wreckage of the overmantel, she wasn't pleased. Out he went into the street, and it was weeks before he was allowed back in the house!

Dirty Blue Knickers

As I grew older, any spare time I had started to feel boring. To fill the hours, I'd find various ways to keep myself entertained. Saturday mornings were particularly busy. If I wasn't playing football for St. Hugh's Central School, I would borrow the milk cart from Coghill's Dairy and head to the gas works in Hind Street. There, I'd load up on six bags of coke at three pence each, which I would then sell for six pence a bag. It was quite a hustle, and I made two trips to the gas works for the coke each Saturday.

Hundreds of people flocked to buy sacks of coke on Saturday mornings, and it was a sight to behold with all the different modes of transport. My milk float was a fine one compared to others—most of the other kids had broken-down prams or makeshift setups constructed from pram bases.

There was one Saturday that I felt the unmistakable sting of my mother's right cross across my face, which felt utterly unfair under the circumstances. It was midday, and I had just wrapped up my Saturday morning rounds at the gas works, distributing bags of coke and pocketing my earnings. I was in high spirits, preparing to give Mam her share of the money and looking forward to a good wash and a change of clothes. The gas works were dirty, and the unpleasant smell lingered in my clothes.

Just as I was about to take off my shirt, a sudden, violent blow to my head sent me reeling sideways—it was Mam's right cross! Before I could regain my balance, another blow from the left side knocked me back. Mam was in a furious mood; apparently, I had been rude to the lady who lived across the street. Unfortunately, this lady and my Mam constantly clashed; their relationship was like a wild cat and a feisty dog, always at odds.

It turned out that I had made some ill-fated remarks to this woman, suggesting that she had been born out of wedlock—though my comments were more crude than that. I had allegedly told her to mind her own business and watch her language, which was shocking to me since I hadn't spoken with her for weeks. There was no point in trying to explain myself to Mam; I knew that further protests would just lead to more punishment. Best to forget it altogether.

My brother Jim, however, didn't see it that way. He told Mam that I had never even spoken to the woman and that I was merely being used as a pawn in this ongoing feud. This only fuelled Mam's anger further—like waving a red flag in front of a bull. She stormed across the road and knocked on the woman's door. According to what I heard afterward, there was quite a scene, and poor Mrs. F ended up flat on her back, revealing her "dirty blue knickers" for the entire neighbourhood to see!

Another incident occurred when Mrs. F visited our house to lay down the law. She marched up the lobby leading from the front door to the living room, with stairs to the bedrooms directly in front. The lino on the floor was polished and incredibly slippery, and as she stood on one of the mats, the tension escalated. After delivering her complaints about Mam, she turned sharply to leave, but her quick movement caused the mat to slip out from under her. With a dramatic flourish, she shot out of the front door onto the pavement, legs kicking in the air, giving all the neighbours yet another good look at her "dirty blue knickers" as she lay there!

Birkenhead Market

"The Market," as it was affectionately called in the North West, was quite large. The Market Hall boasted over 200 stalls and shops, bustling with activity, especially on market days. This vibrant area was located within the main shopping district of Birkenhead, bordered by Market Street, Hamilton Street, Chester Street, and The Haymarket. It opened its doors in 1835 as a fruit and vegetable market and quickly grew in popularity. An extension was added in 1845, and another in 1909, transforming it into a lively hub that attracted more and more visitors.

Beyond the usual market stalls, the atmosphere took on a fairground vibe, complete with swings, roundabouts, beat the goalie, darts, and roll-a-penny, alongside stalls selling sweets, china, lino, carpets, and more. It created a colourful scene that no other Saturday night entertainment could rival.

At the end of the football season, I decided to land a Saturday job at the market. Finding one wasn't easy, but I eventually secured a position with a kindly old man known as "Whisky Bob." I never learned his real name, but he always looked like he needed a shave. Whisky Bob operated two stalls in the fairground area of the market: one for darts and the other for roll-a-penny.

Whenever there was a mishap with the pennies rolling off the counter, I had to crawl under the table to retrieve them, and let me tell you, I didn't enjoy that stall one bit. Thankfully, I was soon promoted to the dart stall: "Three darts for a penny, hit two whites to win!" It was much more challenging than it appeared, and you can bet there were plenty of arguments that surfaced over those games.

Working at the stalls came with its own set of rules—a meal break was unheard of, so Mam would send me off with a flask of tea and some sandwiches. Despite the long hours, I enjoyed my Saturday job and looked forward to it each week, especially since I was earning my own money. My brothers Jim, Frank, and Martin all found work at different stalls too—talk about "Jobs for the boys!" Mam was pleased; she always knew where to find us, and it ensured we wouldn't run into trouble.

While there were a few drunks wandering around in the evenings, I never witnessed any fights or major disturbances. Of course, there were pickpockets, but it was up to each individual to keep an eye on their belongings, and those lessons were best learned quickly.

The market closed at 9:00 p.m., but stalls often ran until around 10:00 p.m. It made for a long, entertaining day. During those hard times in the thirties, the market provided a welcome respite from the daily grind of trying to make ends meet. For that moment, I didn't want to grow up; everything felt just right for me. But I had a nagging feeling that I couldn't expect my idyllic way of life to remain unchanged forever. And grow up I did, but ultimately, everything turned out well for me.

Birkenhead Market late 1950s

The Butcher's Boy

In March 1934, at the age of fourteen, I was finally able to leave school. I applied for jobs at Lever Bros., Woodsons, the Leather Works, and Lewis's Department Stores. Just before Easter, my mother informed me that Reg Johnson, a butcher in the market, needed help for a couple of weeks because his boy had been rushed to the hospital. Excitedly, I accepted the job—after all, I had an order bike to ride around on, and I was getting paid for my work!

I thoroughly enjoyed the role, and Reg taught me a lot about the art of butchery. I learned to carve hindquarters, prepare lamb, pickle beef, link sausages, and handle poultry and rabbits. Reg, being a bit on the lazy side, appreciated my eagerness; the more I did, the less he had to work. My day began at 8:30 a.m. when I opened the stall, prepared orders, and, as soon as Reg arrived, I'd be off on the bike delivering meat to the customers.

Lunch was always at home, and when I returned, Reg would promptly make his way to the pub for a liquid lunch. He would often vanish until around 3:30 p.m., at which point he'd return to the stall for just a short while before heading home. I'd be the one closing up the stall at 5:30 p.m., taking care to secure the takings—a thought that never worried me back then, even though I certainly wouldn't dare to do so today!

Saturdays were particularly busy; I would arrive at the market before 8:00 a.m. and often wouldn't make it home until around 10:00 p.m. Saturday nights were a whirlwind! Back then, most butchers used ice boxes since refrigerators were rare, meaning everyone had to sell out before the market closed. At 8:30 p.m., the first closing bell would ring, signaling the time to start selling off any leftover meat. With about thirty butcher stalls all hustling, regular customers knew the drill and crowded in, creating a bustling atmosphere. It was like a chaotic auction, with customers fighting over the last joint of meat to take home.

Reg's wife was always present on Saturday nights; she was a lovely woman who handled the till while Reg sold the meat, and I would wrap up parcels to pass on to her when customers paid. Once the meat had all been sold, I'd wash up the utensils and help close down for the night. Reg was generous, often giving me a joint and some sausages to take home, and Mam was always eager to see what I brought back!

There were two occasions when I stumbled upon a one-pound note, and both times, I willingly handed them to Reg. After the second find, I told Mam about it, and she advised me, "Next time you find money, you keep it!" Yet, I never encountered more cash.

On another occasion, I went to the bank for change, and to my surprise, I found one pound too much. I asked Reg to double-check, and he confirmed the error. I insisted that I would return it, even though Reg wasn't thrilled with the idea. I went back to the bank, but when I explained the situation, the cashier refused to acknowledge his mistake, clearly reluctant to admit it. Frustrated, I left the bank with the extra pound but never confessed to Reg.

Mondays were reserved for cleaning up; every nook and cranny of the stall was thoroughly scrubbed and polished. It was also the busiest day for the rat collector, as the market's size made rats a constant concern. Each stall set cage traps, and on Mondays, all traps were collected, often yielding five or six rats in each cage, which were dispatched by a couple of feisty fox-terrier dogs.

Next to my stall, a girl named Josie worked, and she was my first girlfriend. Mam and Josie quickly became quite close. I mention Josie because, years later during the war, she experienced a heart-wrenching tragedy—her husband was killed on their wedding day. The couple was celebrating when an air raid occurred, and while many men rushed out to extinguish fires caused by incendiary bombs, Josie's husband didn't make it back home.

As I navigated through life, the Mersey Tunnel had recently opened, and occasionally, I'd ride my bike through it. It was thrilling to bike through the tunnel: two miles downhill and then two miles back up—it certainly kept you fit! My trips were primarily for selling calf hides and rabbit skins, as well as purchasing sausage skins and saltpeter. I always looked forward to my excursions to Liverpool.

However, when the country went to war in September 1939, any plans Birkenhead Council had for revamping the market were put on hold. The air raids during the war caused significant damage to the market, and there was even a fire that broke out in the roof. The bustling atmosphere we once enjoyed began to fade as the war cast a long shadow over our daily lives.

Saturdays at the market lost some of their vibrancy, and the camaraderie that had characterized the bustling stalls started to wane. Many of the familiar faces of vendors and customers alike were replaced by the uncertainty of wartime. The market became a place where tension hung in the air. People were more concerned about the rationing of food and supplies, rather than the delightful offerings that had filled the market stalls in happier times.

Eventually, in the 1960s, the market relocated to its present position in the Grange Road Complex. However, the change was bittersweet. The new modern setup lost the charm and character that had defined the old market. There were no more swings or roundabouts—just a sterile environment that catered to different needs. The bustling atmosphere filled with laughter and shouts of vendors was a distant memory.

The success of the Mersey Tunnel transformed the area entirely, leading to a decline in local shops and market culture. Birkenhead, once a vibrant hub for families like mine, felt the impact of change sweeping through our community.

As I reflect on those days spent working alongside Reg at the butcher's stall, I realize how much they shaped my childhood. The market was more than just a place to work; it was a cornerstone of my youth—an environment rich with lessons, laughter, and the bonds of community. Though times were tough, those experiences carved a place in my heart, serving as reminders of resilience and the simple joys of growing up.

Now, as I walk through the new developments, I can't help but feel a sense of nostalgia for the bustling market where I learned the value of hard work and the importance of community connection. My memories of Birkenhead Market and my youthful adventures remain a cherished part of my story, forever etched in the tapestry of my life.

Scouts

At the age of seven, I joined the Cub Scouts—specifically the 47th Holy Trinity Scout Group. As a Catholic, I faced a bit of a dilemma since there were no Catholic Scout groups in the area around Dacre Street. But I thoroughly enjoyed my three years in the Cubs. That was until a new Vicar rolled into town and declared that all members of the Scouts and Cubs must attend church services. Being a Catholic, I couldn't very well attend services at another church, so I made the tough but ultimately wise decision to leave the Cubs.

In hindsight, it turned out to be a fortunate turn of events. I joined the 1st Birkenhead Scout Group, which was part of the YMCA Troop. One of the big advantages of the YMCA was that it was open every evening—bliss for an energetic lad! The place was filled with activities to keep us entertained: table tennis, billiards, darts, a gym, and more board games than you could shake a stick at. The Scouts even had a Bugle Band, and I proudly took on the role of the bugler. The troop also had a permanent camp site at Irby Mill Hill—what more could an adventurous young boy hope for?

The camp at Irby was fantastic, and we often cycled the six-mile trek to get there. One day, I stumbled upon a Rudge Whitworth upright bike with a three-speed system left outside our house for an entire day. Naturally, being the upstanding citizen I was, I turned it in to the police, completely oblivious to the fact that it might actually become mine.

Months later, I received an official-looking letter from the Birkenhead Police, summoning me to their office in Brandon Street, the head office. My mother was furious, demanding to know what kind of trouble I had gotten into, but I honestly had no clue.

When I arrived at Brandon Street, the Sergeant handed me a slip of paper and ushered me to the lost property office. To my surprise, I discovered the bike was mine to reclaim! The officers congratulated me for my integrity, and I felt like quite the lucky citizen—like I had won the lottery without even buying a ticket! That Rudge Whitworth bike lasted for years, and I was heartbroken when it was eventually gone.

My next bike was more modern, and I felt like a million bucks riding it. However, being a brother comes with its own challenges; my brother Frank took it upon himself to borrow my prized possession without permission for a jaunt to Seacombe. Unfortunately, as luck would have it, he caught his front wheel in a train line over the four bridges at Birkenhead Docks and went flying off the bike. And as if that wasn't enough of a disaster, a train rolled over my bike, leaving me with nothing but fond (and slightly bitter) memories.

As the 1st Birkenhead was the first Scout Troop founded, the original Scout Masters fashioned their own uniforms. We wore wool shirts in plain colours, and instead of the classic neckerchief, we sported green ties—because nothing says "outdoorsy adventures" like feeling slightly like a waiter! The younger Scouts wore short trousers complete with knee-length stockings, while the older Scouts donned long trousers, their shirts decked out with yellow and green braid around the pockets and epaulettes. We believed it made us look quite dapper—until you realized we all patterned our attire after a bag of jelly beans.

The Bugle Band was a highlight, and I took pride in my role as the bugler. We paraded once a month on Sundays, marching through the neighbourhood like we were guarding the Queen. As a Catholic, I had the permanent job of looking after the instruments and equipment—all while trying to squeeze in early Mass. Sometimes I felt like a walking musical instrument rack!

My enthusiasm for Scouting was unwavering; I couldn't help but earn various badges and eventually became a Patrol Leader—because what's more fun than bossing around your friends while camping? In 1936, my efforts culminated in earning the prestigious title of King Scout, the highest award a Scout can achieve—an honour that came with more bragging rights than a trophy!

Lewis's Ltd.

Reg had asked me to stay on his stall until his other boy came back; it was two years later when I finally left the market. The traffic through the Mersey Tunnel was very busy and so the area became very congested. The tunnel was next to the market and trade began to suffer. I realised that there was no future for me in the market and so I applied for a position at Lewis's department store in Liverpool. My cousin, Charlie Johnstone worked there, he told me about the training programme and also about all the lovely girls; hundreds of them he said, but he always did exaggerate.

This is
LEWIS'S
LIVERPOOL'S GREAT STORE

When I reported for work, I was told that the vacancy offered to me (as a Junior Salesman) had not materialised and was asked whether I would be prepared to work in the Bakery until a vacancy arose in the Store. So, I became a became a Junior in the Bakery, cleaning and greasing tins in the bakery and transporting cakes to the Food Department. It was a very physical job but very interesting and it gave me freedom. I would visit the Food Hall, the cafeteria, the three restaurants and the staff dining room. The one drawback was the early start at 7:30 a.m. I would catch the 7:00 a.m. train from Birkenhead, which was far too early for me. Once I got used to it, I found the job had many advantages. In the main, Wednesday was a half-day, so I played football for Lewis's. Occasionally, I had a half-day on Saturday, and then I played for the Birkenhead YMCA.

Lewis's provided all meals for juniors free of charge, the condition was that all juniors had their lunch at 11:30. This was great, all the boys and girls under 18 years of age had their lunch together and, as soon as we finished our lunch, we went up on the roof. It was the usual banter and stupidity of young boys and girls and we liked it, it was the highlight of our day. I was very shy, sort of on the fringe; I was gaining confidence but never knew what to say to these young ladies.

One morning, I was very late arriving at work. My manager, Mr Fussell was a very short-tempered man and, as a punishment, he stopped me from having my lunchtime. I was very upset about this but there was nothing I could do about it. That same day, the staff manager had decided to check on the juniors' behaviour on the roof. It was raining so all the juniors had collected in the corner of the passage leading to the roof. The lights had been switched off, the behaviour of some of the juniors was disgraceful and, consequently, they all lost their jobs. If Mr Fussell had not been so bad-tempered I would have lost my job too. What would I have said to my mother?

On another occasion, I was playing on the roof, we were chasing each other, and I was being chased. To escape the person chasing me, I ran toward the skylights over the restaurants and staff dining room. I jumped over a skylight; at least that was my intention, but my chaser grabbed my jacket as I jumped, and I was arrested in mid-air. I fell through the skylight and landed on the dining table of the "lift girls", beautiful young ladies they were, but I did not stay to say "Hello, just dropping in", I was up and away before they even screamed. I believe a couple of them fainted. I was away like a streak of lightening but, as I ran, I realised that I was bleeding badly so I ran to the Welfare Department on the 5th floor. The nurse was just leaving for her lunch and she was not pleased to see me. "What is your problem?" she asked me. I dropped my trousers and replied, "This is my problem". At first, I think she thought I was being naughty, but when she saw the blood, I thought she was about to faint, but she didn't. She was very efficient, had me bandaged and off to the hospital in record time. The store looked after me exceptionally well, sent me home by taxi, accompanied by one of the Commissioners. When we arrived at our house, my mother was black leading the fireplace, she was in a mess. At first, Mam thought that the Commissioner was a policeman, she was lost for words; the house was in a mess, worse than usual. I was placed on the sofa and the Commissioner could not get away quick enough; he did not know that my Mam was deaf, and she didn't know what had happened. Mam thought that I had fallen off Lewis's roof!

The bakery closed at mid-day on Saturdays. As juniors, three of us had to clean the floor, which we accomplished using a hosepipe. On this particular day, it was warm and sultry, my colleague "Jowler" stood on the window ledge and squirted the hose down on the passing public, who immediately put up their umbrellas. Unfortunately, there happened to be a policeman on point duty who noticed that people were putting their umbrellas up. He looked up and saw Jowler with the hosepipe but, by the time the store security arrived, we had all left the bakery. A full inquiry was held the following Monday morning, but it was all to no avail. Mr Fussell was not convinced of our innocence, he gave severe warnings to nobody in particular, but his eyes never left Jowler.

Shortly after this incident, I was transferred to the Parcels Office. It was shift work; 8:30 a.m. until 5:30 p.m. or 1:30 p.m. until finish, which was normally 9:00 p.m. I found the work easy and interesting; we would be in contact with every department and there was a parcels chute from the 4th floor to the sub-basement, which was great fun. The only problem with the chute was the six foot drop in the sub-basement; a number of boys finished up in the hospital with fractured limbs. On one occasion, I was checking a wrapping a pair of men's shoes and the shoes in the box were very old. I assumed that the customer had decided to wear the new shoes and have the old pair delivered, so I passed them. A few days later, I was sent to the Staff Manager and was basically accused of stealing the shoes. I was bewildered, I could only state that I had assumed the customer had decided to wear the new shoes. I was told to wait outside, the store detective left the office, returned with another junior, and took him into the Staff Manager's office. Shortly after, he came out and told me to return to my Department. It transpired that the detective had remembered seeing the other young man wearing a new pair of shoes. When confronted, the young man admitted his guilt, he was dismissed – I was very relieved.

Occasionally, I would be late arriving for the early shift. We did not clock on, the system was to report to the man in the office at the entrance to the Parcels Office. The old man was almost blind, when you were late, you would creep in underneath his open window, turn around and walk out, making sure that he had seen you. He would always ask the time of your arrival, which was duly noted. On the afternoon shift, one would often find a parcel with a promised delivery on that day. It was too late to be delivered by our van, so the person who lived nearest to the address would deliver the parcel. It was quite a nice little bonus; return fare, early finish and occasionally, a tip from the customer.

I moved on to the Collecting Card Office, which was a promotion for me. It entailed collecting all the customers' purchases, having them packed, and checking the delivery instructions. The odd problem would occur when the customer took the collecting card home instead of leaving it with the assistant or at the Commissioner's Office. This was a very interesting department.

I was transferred again to the Yardage Department, this was my first taste of selling and working closely with the female members of staff. I was very shy and had no conversation with them. My main duties were to keep the stock room clean and tidy and to keep the receiving room clear of our stock. I had to learn how to measure material, how to cut straight lines, plus how to advise on the quantity of material required to make the finished article, bearing in mind the pattern – needless to say, I never mastered that aspect of the job! I was seventeen, allowed to sell and to earn commission but selling yardage was not easy; the female customers did not accept young men serving in that department.

The store models worked in this department, they were beautiful girls. On occasion, they would parade the store wearing beautiful dresses made from our materials. One day, another junior and I mixed up all their clothes into a big heap on the floor, they were furious. They pounced on me, dragged me into the stockroom, gagged me, pulled my trousers down and painted me with red ink. You can imagine the problem I had trying to explain to my mother how I came to have red ink all over my body and underpants!

On the 3rd floor was the Children's Department and a Pets' Corner. There were the usual rabbits, lambs, parrots and fish, plus, on one occasion, there was also a lion, kangaroo, monkeys, and a fountain. The fountain stood in a pool that contained a lot of fish. We found that the source of the water feeding the fountain could be controlled, it was merely a question of finding the switch. The switch was found in the rear of the department; by turning a tap, we could drench the people gazing at the fish. On one occasion, because of our fooling around, the motor burst into flames. I quickly switched the electricity off and the chap with me pressed the fire alarm. By the time the store fire fighters arrived, the whole thing was under control. My friend and I were sent for by the Staff Manager, we thought that we had been seen playing about with the fountain. Imagine our surprise when we were congratulated and awarded one pound each. How could we tell the truth after that?

Shortly after this, I attended my first staff dance. I sat with two other young men; we did not dance, just watched and enjoyed the refreshments. A group of young girls joined us, it was their first dance too. One of the girls lived in Claughton, not too far from where I lived, so I escorted her home. I saw her to her house, then walked through Birkenhead Park. I had a pipe, which I had never smoked, and I thought that this was a good time to try it. I felt quite manly! I was almost out of the park when I suddenly felt very hot and dizzy and I was violently sick. Just through the park was the General Hospital, a couple escorted me to the Casualty Department. I have no idea what treatment they gave me; after a short lie down, I was allowed to go home. I had quite a difficult time trying to explain to my mother that I had come straight home from the dance. I did not attempt to smoke again and I also decided to learn to dance – so some good came out of my first pipe.

My experiences as a junior stood me in good stead when I became the Staff Manager at Lewis's – that was in 1962 – I knew all the old tricks, but the younger generation had also learnt quite a lot of new ones. In one incident, a customer had purchased a pair of shoes over 12 years earlier. He had brought them back, stating that they had not been satisfactory. By a stroke of luck, a retired member of the department was visiting, and she recognised him and told the manager. His claim for a new pair of shoes was refused and he came to the staff office to lodge his complaint. I realised immediately that it was a try-on and, having obtained his name and address, I sent for the complaints book. I checked back and found that he had changed the shoes three times. He threatened to take the matter to his Solicitor, so I thanked him for advising me, and asked if he would be so kind as to let me have his Solicitor's name and address. Of course, he refused, and stormed out of my office, never to be seen again.

On another occasion, a man entered my office and told me that a gang of shoplifters was planning to visit the store. He knew them, the day they would be visiting and knew which departments they would be in. He gave me their names and descriptions, he was so precise, and I was very close to doing a deal with him. I told him that I would have to speak to my General Manager; I did not want to, but he could speak to the GM if he wished. When he refused, I knew it was a ruse to get some money for false information. I left my office and instructed the store detective to have the man followed. In his car we found loads of goods, which he admitted to stealing. Sometimes you can be lucky!

Unfortunately, that day, a keen-eyed policeman on point duty caught sight of the umbrellas rising like an unexpected floral display. He looked up just in time to see Jowler with the hosepipe, but before the store security could intervene, we had all disappeared from the scene. A full inquiry was held the following Monday, but it ended up being for naught. Mr. Fussell was not convinced of our innocence—his glare was enough to make even a saint nervous as he gave vague threats to no one in particular.

Shortly after this escapade, I transferred to the Parcels Office, which felt like a promotion for me. It involved working various shifts—either 8:30 a.m. to 5:30 p.m. or the afternoon shift from 1:30 p.m. until close, which was usually around 9:00 p.m. I found this new role easy and interesting, as it allowed me to interact with every department in the store. We even had a parcels chute that ran from the 4th floor to the sub-basement; let me tell you, it was fun.

The only drawback to the chute was the six-foot drop in the sub-basement; quite a number of boys ended up in the hospital with fractured limbs after miscalculating their landing. One time, I was wrapping up a pair of men's shoes when I came across a very old pair in the box. Assuming the customer wanted to keep the new pair and return the old ones, I passed them along for delivery. A few days later, I found myself called into the Staff Manager's office where I was accused of stealing the shoes! Bewildered, I explained my reasoning, only to be told to wait outside.

A short while later, the store detective emerged with another junior and took him into the Staff Manager's office. I waited anxiously, wondering if I would end up in hot water. Fortunately, it turned out that the detective had recognized the other young man wearing a new pair of shoes when he was recently confronted. When faced with the truth, the young man admitted his guilt, and he was promptly dismissed. I couldn't help but breathe a sigh of relief—one less problem to deal with!

Occasionally, I would arrive late for the early shift. We didn't have to clock in; instead, we reported to a nearly blind old man stationed at the entrance of the Parcels Office. When you were late, you'd sneak in through his open window, turn around to show your face, and then quickly leave, making sure he had seen you. He always asked what time you arrived, diligently noting it down.

During the afternoon shifts, parcels would often arrive with promises for same-day delivery. If it was too late for the van, the nearest boy to the address would be asked to deliver it. It was a nice little bonus—you got the return fare, an early finish, and occasionally a tip from grateful customers.

Eventually, I moved on to the Collecting Card Office, which felt like another promotion. This role involved collecting all of customers' purchases, ensuring everything was packed correctly, and checking the delivery instructions. Occasionally, we faced issues when customers mistakenly took their collecting cards home instead of leaving them with the assistant or at the Commissioner's Office.

Another shift saw me transferred to the Yardage Department, where I had my first taste of selling as well as interacting closely with the female staff. I was painfully shy and had no idea how to strike up a conversation with them. My main duties revolved around keeping the stockroom clean and managing the receiving room's supplies. I had to learn how to measure materials, cut straight lines, and advise customers on the quantity needed for their projects while considering patterns—needless to say, I never quite mastered that part!

At seventeen, I was finally allowed to sell and earn commission, but selling yardage proved to be a challenge; many female customers weren't keen on being served by young men. I often found myself stammering awkwardly while trying to assist them.

The store models, stunning girls dressed in beautiful outfits made from our materials, were a sight to behold. One day, another junior and I mixed up their clothes into a huge pile on the floor, which resulted in pure chaos. You can imagine how furious those models became! They pounced on us, dragged me into the stockroom, gagged me, and painted me with red ink. You can guess how difficult it was to explain to my mother why I had red ink all over my body and underpants!

On the third floor was the Children's Department, which also had a Pets' Corner. There were all the usual animals: rabbits, lambs, parrots, and fish, with the occasional special visitor like a lion, kangaroo, and monkeys, not to mention a fountain that stood in a pool filled with fish. The sheer chaos of managing the animals was both thrilling and challenging, especially for a young lad like me.

One day, while exploring the fountain, we discovered that the water supply could be controlled—it was simply a matter of locating the switch. That switch was tucked away in the back of the department, and we soon figured out that by turning a tap, we could give the unsuspecting visitors a little shower as they gazed at the fish!

Naturally, one fateful day, our playful antics led to trouble. The fountain's motor suddenly burst into flames! Panic ensued, but I quickly switched off the electricity as my partner pressed the fire alarm. By the time the store firefighters arrived, we had managed to get the situation under control, much to their surprise. My friend and I braced ourselves for a serious telling off, expecting the worst. But instead, when we were summoned to the Staff Manager's office, we were greeted with praise and awarded a pound each for our initiative! How could we possibly reveal our true intentions after that?

Occasionally, we would handle special deliveries—like dining suites or three-piece suites that made their way through our doors for "special delivery" on a Friday to impress weekend visitors, only to be returned as "unsuitable" the following Monday. Such was the life in a busy department store!

A History of Lewis's

David Lewis arrived in Liverpool in 1839 at the tender age of 16, having made the journey all the way from America. His mission? To make a fortune through selling. Bright and skilled with figures, he possessed an unwavering determination to succeed. At that time, Liverpool was a bustling city—a major sea port that attracted waves of people from various countries, most of whom were hunting for work. David recognized the opportunity to strike it rich, provided he worked hard—and boy, did he have what it took!

He served his apprenticeship with Benjamin Hyam on Lord Street, and in 1856, he opened a men's clothing shop on Ranelagh Street. Lewis's approach was revolutionary: rather than pricing his goods high and haggling down with customers like every other shopkeeper, he set fixed low prices. This was practically radical at the time! His slogan, "Satisfaction Guaranteed, or Your Money Back," along with his wide range of merchandise, drew in shoppers like bees to honey. His shop was a hit, but as it specialized in menswear, he soon opened a ladies' fashion shop on Bold Street, expanding his empire.

Before long, he had stores in Manchester and Birmingham, solidifying Lewis's stores as a staple for the working class. For years, the Lewis family managed the stores, with help from the Levys and the Cohens. But David determined that fresh ideas were needed. He realized his family couldn't provide the talents required, so he sought out Fredrick Marquis, planning to meet him on a trip across America. Marquis was initially hesitant to join a family business that was 100% Jewish, but he proposed consulting the family. If they agreed, he'd work for a low salary for a three-year trial. Spoiler alert: he stayed!

Marquis's innovative ideas often scared the family. He had a real knack for analysing the needs of both customers and staff. He introduced trade unions to the stores, opened a shoe repair department in the factory, and created a buying office in London. Previously, each department had its own buyer, which resulted in an overwhelming excess of stock. Thanks to Marquis, the selection of one buyer for all stores saved the company thousands of pounds!

Every store employed a Staff Manager responsible for hiring and firing staff, and three councils were established—Sales Managers, Assistant Sales Managers, and Staff councils. The heads of these councils were untouchable during their terms, which must have made for some interesting meetings! Each store boasted a Welfare Department with a trained nurse and even a store doctor, as well as a training department and various facilities designed to support staff. While other organizations criticized Lewis's for being too generous with staff perks, the store saw sales and profits rise, proving everyone wrong.

Lewis's Liverpool Ranellagh st

Before the war, two additional stores opened in Leicester and Hanley, which solidified Lewis's status as one of the major employers in the country. Their policy to purchase for cash and pay suppliers upon return was a stroke of genius, and the introduction of a Lewis's Bank in every store turned out to be a thoroughly appreciated move.

By 1936, Lewis's in Liverpool had claimed its spot as the top store in the area, with Lord Woolton serving as the Managing Director. Whenever Lord Woolton embarked on a train journey, a junior staff member was assigned to retrieve his bag and escort it to the station. The Station Master would typically await our arrival at the main entrance. After the train departed, the junior would scuttle back to the store to report that "Lord Woolton had left by train." As juniors, we couldn't help but find this procedure a bit ludicrous—talk about a royal send-off!

When war broke out in 1939, Lord Woolton, now appointed Minister for the Clothing of the Army, eventually became Minister for Food. He was beloved by housewives throughout the country, which is saying something, as we all know how tough that crowd can be.

I distinctly remember one morning in the Liverpool store around 10:00 a.m. The Biscuit Department had just received a fresh supply of cream biscuits, and a queue formed faster than you could say "chocolate chip." As Lord Woolton strolled through the Food Department, he became the centre of attention. The customers erupted into cheers, serenading him with "For He's a Jolly Good Fellow."

In classic fashion, Lord Woolton called the manager over and declared, "I will not have these good people standing in a queue. Get rid of it." The manager promptly withdrew the biscuits from the counter, and the queue, delighted by the spectacle, erupted in applause before dispersing. I was absolutely astounded! After a reasonable interval, the biscuits returned to the shelves, and lo and behold, the queue reformed—but those who had initially been first were now left at the back!

I still have no idea what the purpose of that exercise was.

Lewis's Junior Camp

Holidays were a luxury that my family and most other juniors didn't often experience. Thankfully, Lewis's organized a junior camp in North Wales, inviting boys from the Liverpool, Manchester, Birmingham, Glasgow, and Leeds stores. For many of us, it was the first time we'd ever been away from home—for an entire week! It was nothing short of fantastic.

My first trip took us to Barmouth, North Wales, where six boys squeezed into a tent—cosy, to say the least! The campsite included a stores tent, a cook's tent, and a mess tent, which made for quite an impressive setup. With boys from all over competing in games and trying to outdo each other, there was never a dull moment! Jack Kirwan and Charlie Ellis, both Senior Managers, organized the entire event, and I made lasting friendships with Harry Davies and Gordon Gregory.

For my second junior camp, we travelled to Abergele. While there, I had my moment of heroism by rescuing two young girls who had gotten into trouble while swimming. I was part of the beach patrol and noticed their plight. I called out to the other boys, but alas, they were either inept at listening or too busy splashing around to pay attention! Jumping into action, I brought the first girl out of the water, and as I turned back to rescue the second, I was feeling pretty worn out. Thankfully, the other boys finally noticed and rushed to help, and together we pulled her to safety. There was an uproar of back-slapping and congratulations from the Senior Managers, who were pleased as punch. The Director of Personnel even showed up to personally commend me, rewarding me with ten shillings—more than a week's wages! When I returned to work, my colleagues in the butcher's stall treated me like a hero.

The camp was a rite of passage. However, when I think back to those girls, I can't help but chuckle at the thought of them let loose in Rhyl—a territory ripe for young troublemakers like us! Every time those girls exited the camp, it felt like a fashion parade; they turned heads. Tearing down the camp meant dismantling many tents and a huge marquee, a laborious task that we managed to finish just before the chaos of breakfast.

Speaking of breakfast, I'll never forget the disaster that struck one morning. Just as we were finishing packing the tents, breakfast was called, and we all gathered for a hearty meal of bacon, eggs, sausages, black pudding, and fried bread. The only hitch? The salt cellar was uncooperative; when the top was on, the salt wouldn't come out, so we decided to remove the lid entirely. Just then, Jack Kirwan came in, rubbing his hands together and declaring what a lovely smell the fried breakfast was. He approached the table, admired his feast, and reached for the salt cellar, shaking it over his breakfast without a second thought. The top fell off, and salt cascaded all over his meal!

There was a stunned silence as Jack's eyes nearly popped out of his head. His face morphed through a spectrum of colours before exploding into a fit of rage directed at whoever left the salt loose. Poor old Charlie Mitchell didn't know how to explain himself and ended up with Jack throwing his breakfast straight into the slops bucket, storming out of the tent. We all swore we would never "pass the salt" again!

The girls we met from Liverpool, Manchester, Birmingham, Glasgow, and Leeds were truly beautiful yet headstrong. Their rivalry only fuelled their antics, and the Territorial Army campers nearby seemed all too willing to encourage their mischief. It wasn't long before the police caught wind of the trouble, which ultimately led to Lewis's Junior Camp closing down.

The Coronation

As a King Scout, I was incredibly fortunate to be selected to attend the Coronation of King George VI in 1936, representing the British Scouting Organization. Our expenses were covered by the Scout Commissioner for Cheshire, Mr. Paul of "Paul Flour Mills," and the wonderful folks at Lewis's graciously gave me the day off work.

We left Birkenhead Woodside at midnight, arriving in London the next morning, where breakfast was served before we collected our lunchboxes. We finally marched to our designated position, arriving around 9:30 a.m., but we didn't leave that spot until 4:00 p.m. It was a day I will never forget! The procession featured the various regiments of the British Empire, an array of royal guests, and, of course, the King and Queen themselves. It was simply fantastic!

Back home, things hadn't changed much. Nanna Kay had moved back in with us, and by this time, I had five brothers under one roof. All of us living together at 64 Dacre Street made for quite a lively household, especially since Dad and Nanna Kay could barely stand to be in the same room together!

Then, out of the blue, Uncle Bob (my mother's brother) returned home after spending over fifteen years in the Army. Despite his presence, I hardly got to know him; my brother Jim was his favourite. Uncle Bob stayed with us for about two years before getting married. After that, he became somewhat of a stranger—his new wife, Mabel, was lovely, but our family dynamic shifted significantly once he settled down.

Reflecting on those busy years, I can't help but recall the bustling life within our home. It was a dance of personalities: my mother's patience (or lack thereof) as she managed us boys, Nanna Kay's strong opinions, and Uncle Bob's sporadic updates on life in the Army. We were a tightly knit crew, though occasionally it felt like a comedy of errors—or perhaps a sitcom waiting to happen!

The Coronation, however, was a defining moment, one of the many extraordinary events that sprinkled my youth with excitement. Watching history unfold before my eyes was a memory to cherish—as was the grand and theatrical atmosphere in which the British people celebrated their royal family. Those times, however tumultuous in our household, were also times filled with moments of pride and community.

With Uncle Bob around, I realized how life continued to change, and as the war approached, a sense of uncertainty began to settle in. The excitement of the Coronation served as a poignant reminder of the joy and tradition that buoyed our spirits during those years. Little did we know that soon, the world outside would shift dramatically, ushering in challenges that would test our resilience and bond as a family.

And so, within the walls of our home in Dacre Street, we continued to navigate the complexities of family life, the whimsical joys of our youthful pursuits, and the looming spectre of a world at war. Each day unfolded with its own adventures, lessons, and the undeniable love that held us all together, guiding us through the trials ahead.

Mam

My mother, Charlotte—affectionately known as "Lottie"—was a truly wonderful woman. With her ever-present smile, she had a way of making everyone feel happy just by being around her. People would often say they felt better after talking to Lottie, and I couldn't agree more. Although life dealt her some tough cards, she never complained. Her deafness sometimes meant she missed parts of conversations, but with her keen ability to lip-read, it was never obvious.

Mam was no fool; she knew every trick in the book and made sure we never dared to tell her lies or disobey her. As I've mentioned before, Nanna Kay was a striking woman, and so was my mother—tall, with dark hair and a lovely face that could light up the room.

Children? Oh, Mam had plenty of us! Money, on the other hand, was in short supply. There were good times when work and overtime came rolling in, but those moments were few and far between. Yet, despite the struggles, Mam's sense of humour was truly contagious. Unfortunately, that didn't always sit well with Dad. He was a bit of a miser, and I suppose he felt overshadowed by her popularity, which led him to indulge in the two main pastimes of married men: drinking and betting on horse racing. Oddly enough, even though he was out of work more often than in, we never went without. I did all the things my friends did, while their fathers had steady jobs.

The Byrne family of 9 boys (Left to Right)

Frank, Alan, Tom, James Byrne, Stephen, Lottie, Gerald, Raymond, Martin, Jim, Jack (me)

One of Mam's biggest worries was the fear of any of her sons getting into trouble. She instilled a healthy fear of the police in us. My brother Martin spent several years in the hospital and at Thingwall Convalescent Home after contracting tuberculous bone disease in his leg. Losing those early years of schooling meant that he had to work harder than any of us to catch up.

When Martin was under five, he developed a peculiar fondness for getting "lost," particularly during trips to Liverpool or Grange Road. What was Martin's escape route? He loved being taken to the police station! There, he'd be treated to a cup of tea, a cake, and sometimes even a penny or two, all before being escorted back home in a police car. As you can imagine, this didn't go over well with Mam when it happened! But for Martin, it was all part of the fun.

He always had a plausible story ready about how he found himself wandering and how lucky he was to end up at the police station. His tales usually concluded with the dramatic revelation, "You know, Mam; I could have been stolen and taken aboard a ship!" And every time, he somehow managed to charm his way out of trouble!

The Cocky Rabbit

After my unfortunate plunge through the skylight over the staff dining room at Lewis's, I found myself laid up at home with numerous stitches in my right leg, running from just below the knee to almost around the ligament behind my knee. Thankfully, I had been lucky—it was just a flesh wound. Still, being "laid up" meant I couldn't move around much, and boredom quickly set in. I needed a distraction, and that's when I spotted a wooden box waiting to be chopped up for firewood. Suddenly, a brilliant idea struck me—I could transform that box into a rabbit hutch! After all, rabbits were sold every Saturday at Birkenhead Market, and I could have one to keep.

Taking my time over two days, I converted the box into a fully functional rabbit hutch. My brothers gathered straw and food, and Saturday became the big day for our furry new resident. I passed my brother Frank some cash for the rabbit, instructing him to make sure it was a doe. As I waited with eager anticipation, I grew worried when an hour passed without his return. How hard could it be to buy a rabbit? The market was merely five minutes away, and several of my pals had gone with him!

Just when I was about to send out a search party, my mother took an interest and declared her intention to check on Frank herself. She was just pulling on her coat when a knock at the front door announced Tommy Francis. I couldn't hear the conversation between Mam and Tommy, but I eagerly awaited Mam's re-entry, carrying a carrier bag. When she did come back inside, Tommy explained that there were no rabbits for sale that day. Instead, the man in charge had convinced Frank to buy something else.

With that, Tommy reached into the bag and pulled out a little cockerel. I was flabbergasted! What on earth could I do with a cockerel? I had been banking on a cute little rabbit, not a feathered fiend!

With Mam now busy, Tommy seemed at a loss for what to say or do. "Put the cockerel in the hutch," I suggested, but the thought of housing a cockerel in a rabbit hutch was both ridiculous and entertaining!

In the days that followed, Frank cleverly avoided me. Surprisingly, I grew fond of the little guy and realized I had to create a roosting perch for him. The cockerel seemed to take up residence in the makeshift hutch and claimed our backyard as his kingdom. At first, he was cautious of cats, but soon enough, the tables turned—the cats seemed more afraid of him! Poor neighbours complained about him launching surprise attacks on their legs as they headed down the yard to use the toilet. He became notorious for flying up to any open window and barging in, ready to rule the inside as well!

Eventually, it became clear that our feathery friend would need to go. His crowing at dawn was far from welcome, and while it was easy to say he had to go, deciding how to dispose of him proved a bit more difficult.

At that time, work at the docks was scarce, and Dad had been out of a job for a while. Someone suggested that our cockerel would make a fine

Sunday dinner for the family. The only problem? Who would do the deed? Naturally, it fell to me. Now, fully back at work and tied up on Saturdays, I would have to carry out the messy execution on Sunday morning after Mass.

So, on Sunday morning at 11:30, my brothers and I readied ourselves for the cockerel's demise. Frank was to hold the bird down, Jim was tasked with holding its head, and I was designated as the one wielding the axe—my hands were shaking like leaves in a storm! Ironically, Jim seemed more frightened of me with the axe than of the bird itself.

Once we were set, I lined up the axe at the back of the bird's neck, took a deep breath, and swung hard. In one swift stroke, chaos erupted! There was a loud squawk, and blood went spraying everywhere. The severed head continued to squawk, while the headless cockerel ran around in frantic circles. We immediately dashed into the house—what a mess!

Of course, my brothers flatly refused to help clean up the blood; it was left to me to tackle the aftermath. It took ages, and inevitably, my favourite shirt ended up covered in blood. I didn't notice this until I handed Mam the headless chicken. I didn't think I'd enjoy my chicken dinner, but to my surprise, it actually turned out quite tasty—much better than rabbit!

New Year's Eve 1936

New Year's Eve, 1936—it feels like a lifetime ago, doesn't it? Back then, celebrations were a far cry from the extravagance we often see today. Most people enjoyed the early evening at home with family and friends, and if you were under eighteen, good luck getting into a pub! Pubs were basically the exclusive domain of men, leaving young lads like me to kick off the evening with our families before making our way to the Town Centre. For me, that meant Charing Cross.

Charing Cross was bustling, with five roads leading into it, one of which was Grange Road, the main shopping strip of Birkenhead. There was very little traffic that night, and what traffic there was got expertly diverted by the police. By the time we arrived, the air was alive with music and laughter. People paraded around, playing their instruments—be it accordion, banjo, mouth organ, or violin—and the noise was infectious. Fancy dress costumes were all the rage; street musicians were surrounded by joyous circles of dancers singing and laughing, creating a scene straight out of a festive postcard.

At 10:00 p.m., the pubs would close, suddenly doubling the size of the crowd and the noise level! While the male voices added a raucous, off-key flair to the singing, the joyful chaos only enhanced the merriment.

Shortly before midnight, people joined hands for "Auld Lang Syne," bidding farewell to the old year. A maroon was fired from the docks, ringing in the new year. As the Town Hall Clock struck its first ring, the remainder of the bells went unheard amid the festivities. Every ship on the river and in the docks blared their sirens and hooters, blending together into a symphony of celebration. The sheer volume of cheering and singing made it impossible to single out any one noise; it was absolutely fabulous!

In 1936, I was a proud member of the 1st Birkenhead Scouts, the YMCA group. Our Scout Master, John Duddleston, proposed that we hike to Moreton Cross for New Year's Eve. Now, Moreton is about six miles away, but the thought of an adventure excited us. I can't recall how many turned up for the trip, but I remember Bill Forrester, Fred Sessford, Jack McKinlay, and Harold Brookes being there, along with many others whose names slipped my mind over the years.

We arrived at Moreton just before 10:00 p.m. to find that John had arranged a delicious fish and chip supper along with lemonade—what a splendid idea! After a meal that rivalled a banquet in the eyes of hungry boys, we made our way to Moreton Cross. It was similar to Charing Cross, just on a much smaller scale; at that time, Moreton was more of a quaint village. The celebratory atmosphere was wonderfully familiar; the maroon from the river set all the church bells ringing, and the sounds of hooters and sirens echoed around us. With so many bells surrounding the cross, their chimes were truly beautiful.

We mingled with the revellers, swept up in a sea of laughter and song—it was chaotic and magical all at once. As the excitement waned, we gathered ourselves together and started the long walk home. We sang songs along the way, but our energy had been spent, and all we wanted was to get home to our warm beds.

It must have been around 3:00 a.m. when I finally arrived home. As usual, Mam was curled up asleep on the couch, refusing to go to bed until all of her brood was safely inside. When I walked in, she stirred awake, and I eagerly regaled her with tales of my evening. She loved hearing about it and fondly reminisced about similar joyous occasions before she was married.

I made a promise to Mam right then and there: when I married, I would always celebrate Christmas and New Year with my family. Fortunately, so far, I've held true to that promise.

To this day on Christmas Day, we invite all our friends and their children over for drinks, and Father Christmas always makes an appearance with small gifts for the kids. New Year's Eve typically finds us at the Golf Club Dinner Dance, followed by a return to McMasters (our Scottish friends). No one enters the house until I "let the New Year in," a lovely tradition that everyone enjoyed.

Time marches on, and I can't help but reflect on the fact that some of our friends are no longer with us. Yet, Christmas and New Year remain the highlights of the year, and I hope they continue to be so for many more years to come—even if I'll be turning 76 in March! Here's to hoping age really is just a number, right

The Chalet

My job at Lewis's quickly shifted gears, and I found myself dealing in furniture. Now, selling furniture was a whole different ballgame compared to meat or cakes. You had to be well-versed in your merchandise, knowing everything from the manufacturers to the range of colours and stains available, plus the stock lurking in the warehouse. If an item was out of stock, I had to inform customers how long the replacements would take and keep track of our delivery schedule. The commission was just a puny penny for every pound sold; not much by today's standards, but I was determined to make at least a pound a week.

Around this time, I was also navigating a crossroads in my Scouting career. After four years in the 1st Birkenhead Scouts (the YMCA troop), and now at sixteen, I felt it was time for a change. I explored other organizations, but ultimately, I couldn't see past the joys and satisfaction of our weekend camping trips. Plus, the YMCA was open every evening, which meant plenty of opportunities for mischief!

Then, out of the blue, the Scouting Authority in Cheshire announced that the 1st Birkenhead Scout Group would need to comply with the new "Scouts Dress Regulations." This meant a complete overhaul of our uniforms. Gone were our beloved shirts; we now had to wear ones with gold braid on the epaulettes and pockets, ties instead of neckerchiefs, and long trousers instead of shorts. The price of a new uniform was far beyond my budget, and many of us found the change too drastic. Thus, the era of the 1st Birkenhead Scouts came to an unfortunate end.

This departure stung. We had camped every weekend from April through October at our cherished site at Irby-Mill-Hill, just across from Lumden's Café, which still looks the same today. Luckily, our group's eldest member, Harold Brookes, heard that an empty chalet in Dodd's Wood was available for rent. After contacting the Dodds, we secured it for just 7 shillings and 6 pence a week! The chalet was a dream, boasting three bedrooms, a spacious lounge, and a kitchen—though the toilet was, of course, outside. It became our perfect hideaway.

Because of my job at Lewis's, I was responsible for supplying pots, pans, crockery, cooking utensils, and cutlery. Luckily for me, there was a sale in the household department, and I made off with some fabulous deals using my staff discount. We even had a large table made out of a solid piece of wood resting on trestles, big enough for all six of us to feast around.

While I worked Saturdays until 6:00 p.m., I would make a frantic dash home to change, grab a bite to eat, and then cycle the seven or eight miles to Irby. By the time I arrived, the gang would usually already be out, but they'd leave me a note detailing where to find them. Sometimes I'd join in their escapades, but more often, I stayed in the chalet to whip up supper, eagerly awaiting their return around 10:30 p.m.

One extra advantage of the chalet was that my mother often spent time there with my younger brothers; it was a wonderful tonic for her. Mam would head to the chalet on Monday and come back on Thursday.

Inside the chalet, we'd play cards for matchsticks; that was our stake money, and I had a classic move up my sleeve. Dressed in our woollen pullovers, I would slyly use my sleeve to swipe matchsticks from the other players. "Hey, Fred Sessford!" I'd say with mock innocence, "What's that I see behind you?" As Fred ranted and raved, threatening to "bat my eye in," I'd chuckle, realizing he was more likely to have a heart attack from all that fuss than actually land a blow. I often wondered what it would feel like to have my "eye battered in"—not that I wanted to find out!

Sunday mornings were much like those spent at Scout Camp. I'd rise early and head off to church, and when I returned, there was always breakfast waiting for me. The gang would then head off to their church service as I tidied the chalet and prepared dinner. After we filled our bellies, we often hopped on our bikes for a ride to Meols or West Kirby. Sometimes, we would indulge in a game of Pitch and Putt, but I always enjoyed the walk through Thurstaston Woods and over the hill. There were always so many different activities to keep us occupied. On Sunday nights, we played cards or engaged in friendly discussions, then it was an early bedtime to get ready for the coming week. Monday mornings saw us cycling home, changing our clothes, and heading off to work, refreshed and ready to take on whatever lay ahead.

One incident that stands out clearly in my mind was the infamous "Big Toe" episode. It all began one fateful day on the football field. I was taking a free kick when, in an unfortunate turn of fate, I kicked the frozen ground, propelling my big toenail into the bone. The pain shot through me, and I was rushed to the hospital where they had to remove the first joint of my big toe! They wrapped it in a Vaseline bandage and instructed me to keep it on for four weeks.

Two weeks later, I made the trek to the chalet, blissfully unaware of the chaos that awaited me. On Sunday morning, I walked into the chalet to a dreadful smell that immediately aroused suspicion. I was promptly blamed for it, forced to sleep in a small room with my foot propped by the open window—not exactly a comfortable position!

When the smell lingered the following weekend, I was once again the recipient of the blame. But I knew it wasn't me; I had been at home all week, and there had been no foul odour there! Determined to uncover the source, I decided to clear out the room and give it a good clean. When I moved my camp bed aside, I discovered the source of the stink—the cat had given birth to four kittens that didn't make it, and they were indeed covered in maggots.

The gang, already embarrassed by their misjudgements, swung into action and helped clean the room out, though I couldn't help but think they should have known better! On the bright side, I was rewarded with an extra slice of cake with my tea as a consolation!

The YMCA became a hub for young men, and it was there that our interests in girls blossomed. The Amateur Dramatics and the gym sessions introduced us to the opposite sex. The YM had a café that the girls frequented after their practices, where they would sit together as a group, while we young men gathered in our own little huddle, pretending to be cool and collected.

Gradually, we learned their names and started chatting with them. As far as I know, no romances truly blossomed from those encounters, but we certainly became more aware of girls and took a bit more care in our appearance. I could never muster the right words; the girls in the Amateur Dramatics never stopped talking, so I often found myself just sitting back, listening to their dramatic tales.

After the war, we held out a glimmer of hope to return to our cherished chalet—only to discover that all was lost. It was gone, along with all our furniture, crockery, and beloved utensils. I was particularly heartbroken over the special table, large enough to accommodate all of us, which had cost us a whopping one pound, six shillings, and eight pence!

The War Years

Scousers

Anyone born and raised in Liverpool or Birkenhead is proudly dubbed a "Scouser." Most of them possess a tremendous sense of humour, often self-deprecating, turning everyday occurrences into a punchline. They've perfected the art of telling whimsical stories about the absurdities of life—whether they're true or exaggerated for effect—leaving you in stitches and completely charmed. It's their unique way of welcoming you into their world, expecting you to share a light hearted history of yourself in return. However, if you dared to impress them with tales of your own life, you'd swiftly find yourself looking like a fool and cut off from the friendship of these witty Scousers. Under the right circumstances, they could be a bit vicious, but their pride in being Scouse ran deep, and nobody defended their name like they did!

Over the years, many Scousers have made a name for themselves in the boxing world, with legends like Nel Tarleton and Dom Volant. The armed forces also enjoyed their fair share of Scouse talent, as did radio and television—think Arthur Askey, Tommy Handley, Ted Ray, Jimmy Tarbuck, and Ken Dodd. Not to mention sports; whether it was football, cricket, rugby, or tennis, you name it, they had done it. And how could I forget to mention The Beatles? Mersey Beat, and all that!

But the Scousers faced their fair share of challenges during the war. The Germans seemed determined to obliterate Liverpool and Birkenhead, throwing everything including the kitchen sink at us—thousands of bombs littered the city and its suburbs. There were incendiary bombs to set buildings ablaze and high explosives to turn neighbourhoods into rubble. But they failed to extinguish the indomitable spirit of the Scousers. In fact, their efforts only fuelled a greater determination among the locals to win the war. Even the dock laborers pledged no more strikes until we had beaten the Germans, working tirelessly, 24 hours a day, to ensure our troops overseas had everything they needed to fight. The shipbuilders, factory workers, firefighters, nurses, ambulance men, policemen, and, of course, the unsung housewives held everything together—without them, the enemy could never break that spirit.

The Mersey Docks buzzed with activity during the war years. Liverpool was a vital port, with most cargo ships docking at either Liverpool or the Birkenhead docks. Large ships regularly anchored while waiting to enter the docks. In peacetime, dock workers were a volatile bunch; strikes could erupt at a moment's notice. In fact, most of the time, the men didn't even know why they were on strike—it was like a competition to see who could be the loudest rabble-rouser. Birkenhead dockers were generally more controlled than their Liverpool counterparts; the majority lived in the Parish of St. Lawrence's Church, where their Trade Union was strong..

One significant problem faced by Liverpool—being such a large seaport—was the ease with which a married man could abandon his wife and family for a life at sea. Eventually, he'd return, showering his children with gifts and handing his wife a small sum of money, all while claiming he was trying to secure a better life for them. Meanwhile, the only "gift" she often received was another surprise pregnancy! Poverty was rampant, and in their struggles, families banded together to support one another. In our world, the mother was always the mainstay of the home.

The area where I was born and lived for 26 years has since been demolished and rebuilt, with only one of the gang members, Bill Forrester, still around.

After the war, dockers returned to their notoriously volatile ways, unwilling to accept that the world had moved on. The docks on the Continent attracted trade due to their lower costs and greater reliability. The Liverpool dockers had to start from scratch, working hard to regain the trust of shipowners—a task they managed to achieve eventually, although they had to accept whatever conditions the shipping companies laid down.

Joining Up – October 1939

In 1938, the Militia was established, meaning that any male aged twenty would be called up for two years of military service. The first to go, Jack McKinlay, was called up immediately. At that time, war seemed like a distant thought—we were more concerned about school and the latest football match than the looming clouds of conflict on the continent. Jack remained in the military until 1946, rising through the ranks to become a Warrant Officer Class 2 Company Sergeant Major.

At the time of Jack's call-up, most of us were oblivious to the coming war; we merely fretted over how it might impact our careers. We continued our weekly routine of working during the week and heading off to the chalet on weekends, blissfully unaware that the crisis in Europe was escalating beyond our comprehension.

I will always remember Sunday, September 3, 1939. I was alone at the chalet while the others attended church in Irby Village (I had already been to the 9 o'clock Mass in Heswall). While I had the wireless on, Big Ben chimed eleven o'clock, and then Prime Minister Neville Chamberlain announced to the nation that we were at war with Germany. I sat there, feeling numb, completely unable to grasp why we were going to war.

When the gang returned from church, we huddled together and talked it over, but in the end, we still had no real understanding of what it all meant. However, we all agreed that we would join up as soon as possible. Our brave idea to enlist in the Army was soon knocked on the head; the Army was in the midst of calling back the reserves. We ended up twiddling our thumbs until October before we could officially volunteer.

Bill Yates, Fred Sessford, and I decided that we needed to get the ball rolling and headed to the recruitment office in Liverpool the very next day. We didn't want to wait around for the call-up; after all, I could have ended up in the Salvation Army! In a moment of high ambition and youthful bravado, we decided to join The Grenadier Guards.

We hadn't considered that Fred Sessford was still an apprentice, meaning he had to join the Royal Engineers instead. Ironically, Fred eventually became a Sergeant, proving that life has its quirks. Bill and I enrolled in The Grenadier Guards with me assigned number 2616748 and Bill with 2616749. At the time, we couldn't have cared less about the numbers—they felt meaningless. But soon enough, we learned that a lower number meant seniority, which quickly became a running joke between us.

When we enlisted, I was in front of Bill. My interview went smoothly until they asked for my date of birth. I truthfully replied, "21st March 1920." Unfortunately, at just 19 years old, I was too young to enlist. The Sergeant instructed me to come back when I was 20. So, like any clever lad trying to fast-track his way into the Army, I took a stroll around the block, then returned to the recruiting office, standing right back in front of the same Sergeant as if I were a brand new recruit!

I repeated my answers but slyly adjusted my date of birth to 5th October 1919. I was sworn in without a hitch—I was officially in the Army!

I then headed to Lewis's to speak with Mr. Gamble, the Staff Manager. He advised me to stay at work until I received my reporting instructions, which I dutifully followed. Two weeks later, my papers arrived. Bill Yates received his papers at the same time, and we travelled down to London together, sharing a train car filled with men who had also been called up or were recruits like us. The new recruits were easily distinguishable; they all clutched suitcases or large paper parcels from home.

The organization at Euston Station was impressive. Before long, we found ourselves headed to the Guards Depot at Caterham. The depot was conveniently located next to a lunatic asylum, which wasn't lost on us; the noise and chaos of the Guards Depot made the asylum sound positively peaceful! Every recruit yearned for a moment of tranquillity in those early days.

Upon our arrival, we debussed just inside the gate at Caterham, where a Sentry stood as still as a statue. A Sergeant quickly grouped us together before a Senior NCO arrived on the scene. He bellowed, "Form up in Three Ranks!" Confused, we exchanged glances; none of us had a clue what "Three Ranks" meant. There were about thirty of us, varied by our orientation to military service—some packed suitcases, some clutched brown paper parcels.

The next three days were a whirlwind of activity— Go! Go! Go! We were ushered through a chaotic frenzy of collecting our kit and clothing. Let me tell you, it was like a game of musical chairs but with a lot more shouting and a lot less music. I was lucky; my uniform fit quite well, but I felt bad for some of the lads who looked like they had been dressed by blindfolded tailors! The atmosphere was filled with noise, pushing, and rushing, yet somehow, after three days, we all emerged looking like soldiers—though the "square bashing" was just around the corner.

No one could truly prepare us for the physical and mental challenges we were about to face as recruits. The NCOs at the Guards Training Depot showed no mercy. The shouting and stomping of feet echoed through the halls from 6:30 a.m. until lights out at 10:00 p.m. Even the time of day was transformed into a military operation; 4 o'clock in the afternoon became "16:00 hours," causing more confusion than I thought possible!

Cakes became "wads," tea morphed into "char," and our pyjamas turned into polishing rags for our webbing and boots. It was amazing how quickly you learned to overlook the joys of civilian life!

Each squad had a "Trained Soldier," a seasoned member of the Grenadier Guards who bore the immense responsibility of educating the recruits on the regiment's history and instilling proper uniform standards. Above every bed in the barrack room hung a "Battle Honour" won by the Regiment. Woe betide anyone who failed to remember the details of the battle honour above their bed!

The training period lasted 12 weeks, and it was no walk in the park. When I enlisted, I thought I was fit and healthy. Those twelve weeks quickly taught me a stark lesson about my own limitations and vulnerabilities. As recruits, we were confined to the depot for those 12 weeks, unable to leave until we passed the "Passing Out Parade," proving we could walk, salute, and conduct ourselves as proper Guardsmen. We were all eagerly anticipating the day we could step out and see Caterham, but that was not to be—we passed out and were immediately stationed at Chelsea Barracks.

Now in London, I quickly realized just how expensive the city was! Thankfully, Bill Yates's sister lived nearby; she was married to a policeman who hadn't received his call-up yet. Bill and I cherished our weekends spent away from barracks, visiting his sister and her husband. They provided the comforting ambiance of a lovely home where we could finally kick off our Army boots and forget about our military drills for a bit.

The main issue for Bill and me was our surnames! His last name being Yates meant he was always at the end of the roll, while I was at the beginning. Our differing placements often kept us apart, meaning I found myself wandering around Chelsea on my own. And let me tell you, wandering Chelsea in December/January wasn't exactly thrilling!

Byrne the Boxer

During our time at Chelsea Barracks, my squad was stationed on the third floor—a terrible climb after three long hours of training. Our regime included weapon training, using rifles, Bren guns, bayonets, and rigorous foot drills. Saturday mornings were reserved for "Swank Parade." Little did we know that we were unknowingly practicing for "Trooping the Colour," a drill we would repeat time and again, even during our later deployments in Tunisia, Italy, and Austria.

It was during my tenure at Chelsea that I had my first taste of boxing. Reveillé blasted at 6:30 a.m., and the race against time began! The routine was to leap out of bed, dress quickly, make our beds, and then pull our beds away from the wall to allow "The Swab" of the day to scrub behind them. After a quick wash and shave, we stood ready for "Breakfast Parade," which followed half an hour later.

On one particular morning, however, I overslept and didn't jump out of bed at 6:30 a.m. Instead, I lay lazily in my bunk, acutely aware that my fellow recruits were busily pulling their beds away from the wall around me. Realizing I was late, I bolted upright, threw on my shirt, and dragged my bed out. To my horror, the rifle belonging to the man in the next bed slipped to the floor; he had clearly neglected to secure it in the rifle rack!

This chap was the bully type, hailing from Birmingham, and he had two brothers who were professional boxers. "Pick my rifle up!" he yelled, exuberantly sprinkled with choice expletives. I couldn't be bothered and told him to pick it up himself. With threats of violence in the air, he advanced, throwing a punch that I narrowly dodged. In a surprising twist, I managed to land a solid hit right on his jaw. He stumbled, losing his balance and crashing across my bed, landing face down on the floor. Just as the dust settled, the Squad Sergeant strutted into the room, and all he saw was Guardsman Brady sprawled out on the ground. Naturally, he could hear the cheers of approval from the rest of the squad echoing around the barracks.

In the blink of an eye, I found myself sandwiched between two other Guardsmen and was swiftly rushed into close-arrest. Before I could even grab my uniform, I was marched into the Guardroom wearing nothing but my shirt and underpants—what a glamorous look! I was officially on a charge: "Whiles on active service fighting!" At 8:45 a.m., I was scheduled to attend the Commanding Officer's Memoranda; I could only wonder how this circus would play out.

Fortunately, my clothes were brought to me while I was waiting. For reasons beyond my understanding, the CO's Memoranda was cancelled, and I was released from my "open arrest." Talk about dodging a bullet!

Dinner that day was at 12:30 p.m.—and what a meal it was! We dined on rabbit pie, potatoes and peas, followed by spotted dick (yes, the name raised a few eyebrows!). As we neared the end of our meal, the officer of the day asked, "Any complaints?" When no one replied, it was understood to mean "no complaints." Then the Sergeant Major entered, called us to attention, and announced that the Grenadiers would be boxing against the Scots Guards that evening.

Unfortunately, there were two spots that needed filling: one for a boxer weighing in at 10 stone and another at 11 stone. To my surprise, a lad stood up—he was 10 stone—but no one else volunteered. "Now then, where is Guardsman Byrne? I believe he can use his fists!" Well, I had to pipe up and reveal that I was, unfortunately, the 11 stone contender. I was told to report to the gym at 2:30 p.m. for the weigh-in.

Arriving at the gym at 2:30, I was weighed and discovered I was 2 pounds over the middleweight limit. My rabbit pie and spotted dick had clearly left their mark! I spent the next two hours sweating it out to drop those extra pounds. When I finally emerged from that ordeal, I was decked out in fencing gear, complete with the face mask to protect my delicate features.

After what felt like an eternity, I staggered back to the barrack room, flopped onto my bed, and fell into a deep sleep—thank goodness! It felt like just moments later when I was rudely awakened and ordered to don my gym kit, overcoat, and towel. I made my way to the gym, feeling like a deer caught in headlights. The other boxers were already warming up and seemed to know the drill well, while I was left hanging around like a spare part.

Finally, after what felt like hours of anxious waiting, I was called to the ring. As I walked down the aisle, everything appeared dazzling white, and I could feel all eyes on me. A Sergeant leaned over from his seat and whispered, "Watch him—Brigade Champion Egypt." I was so dazed at that moment that I didn't quite grasp what he meant.

When I climbed into the ring, I found myself opposite a giant of a man, a veritable mountain with a bronzed physique and massive tattoos adorning his arms. My "second" was a Sergeant I had never seen before—great, just what I needed! He offered little guidance as I tried to steel myself for the bout. The bell rang, and we advanced to the centre. The Sergeant in charge muttered a few instructions that flew over my head, then said, "Back to your corners, come out fighting on the bell!"

As the bell rang, I surged forward, only to be met with a savage left hook that I clearly should have seen coming. He caught me right on the Adam's apple—a cardinal sin in boxing! You're supposed to keep your chin down on your chest to guard it, but there I was, trying to cough and check if I was still alive while figuring out how to exit that ring without looking like a complete fool. My opponent, sensing easy prey, began parading around me while throwing lefts and rights so fast that I couldn't see them, but oh, I could certainly feel them!

The bell sounded, signalling the end of Round One. There was a palpable silence from my squad while the Scots Guards erupted into uproarious cheers. My second leaned in and said, "You can take everything he throws at you; just give him a good right to the chin.

With renewed determination, the bell rang for Round Two, and I charged across the ring almost before he had the chance to stand up. I threw a right jab just under his heart, and to my surprise, I heard him gasp as all the wind was knocked out of him. Seizing the moment, I followed up with a solid left hook straight to his chin. He crashed to the canvas and was out like a light!

The cheers erupted from the Grenadiers, stamping their feet in celebration, while the Scots Guards sat in stunned silence. I had managed to turn the tide in our favour! Who knew that my short stay at Lewis's and all those summers spent playing on the streets would one day lead me to knock out a giant in the boxing ring?

The next morning, however, I had to attend the Commanding Officer's Memoranda. Marching in with my cap off, I fully expected to face the charge of "fighting in the barrack room." Instead, the CO looked me up and down and said, "Well done, Byrne—here's your prize!" To my astonishment, I was handed a voucher for 7 shillings and 6 pence to be spent in the NAAFI. I never even learned the name of my opponent, but I was fortunate enough to be transferred to the Training Battalion at Windsor the very next day. It turned out that the officers had made a decent sum wagering on our match, and my victory had clinched their win.

I later discovered that the PTO Sergeant, the one who had put me through two hours of hell in the gym, was also the second to my opponent. Thankfully, I never had to face him again!

Windsor Barracks

I hardly had time to settle into life at Windsor before I was granted five days of leave—my first taste of freedom! Unfortunately, the weather was dreadful; it had been snowing for almost a week. I thought I was fit and ready for anything, but after a few days at home, I caught the flu, which left me unfit to travel back to the barracks, according to our family doctor.

Two Military Policemen arrived at our house to escort me to Lime Street Railway Station, where I boarded a train to Euston Station and then transferred to Waterloo Station en route to Windsor. Upon arrival, I was placed in close arrest and spent the night in the guardroom. The next morning, I was released into "open arrest" and informed that I would be boxing that very night!

Fight night came, and to my surprise, I won! I received another voucher for 7 shillings and 6 pence—was this making me a professional boxer? Perhaps I could start charging for autographs! The charges of being "absent without leave" were mysteriously dropped, and I walked away with a sense of triumph.

Every Saturday morning, we had a cross-country run, and the first leg of the race was known as the "Mad Mile." We would start from the barracks, run through Windsor Park to the statue, and then cut cross-country through the Eton School grounds and back to Windsor, totalling about three miles. There was a chap named Roberts, a cross-country expert who ran for the Berkshire Club, and I made it my mission to keep him in sight.

As we came back into Windsor along Epsom Road, I realized that Roberts and I had left the pack far behind. Just as we passed Windsor Castle, Roberts picked up his pace and, to my chagrin, left me in the dust. I finished the run in second place, a few minutes behind Roberts. I promised myself I would beat him the next Saturday, but alas, I tried three times and came in second once and third twice. Roberts eventually rose in the ranks, becoming a Sergeant in the 3rd Battalion. Later, he was wounded in North Africa, and I helped carry him off the battlefield—a small payback for all those runs!

In 1940, with the Royal Family spending much of their time at Windsor Castle, guard duty became particularly strict. The two princesses enjoyed walking past the sentries just to watch them "Present Arms"—but this practice changed when a new order arrived stating that sentries only had to "Present Arms" once to any member of the Royal Family. Now that was the first sensible order I'd heard in the Army!

Typically, I pulled double sentry duties alongside Vic Adams or James Bond, who was a character in his own right. If there was trouble brewing, you could bet James Bond would be at the centre of it!

One particularly cold night in January, Bond and I were on duty from midnight until 2:00 a.m. on posts six and seven, overlooking the east lawn. Just as our breath turned to frost, I heard shots ring out from Bond's position. I dropped to one knee, cocked my rifle, and scanned the lawn for any signs of trouble. I didn't see an intruder, but I heard two more shots and rushed over to Bond.

Best Friends Vic Adams and me

He explained that he had seen figures moving across the lawn, called out a challenge, and then opened fire when he didn't receive a response. You see, during that time, the IRA were quite active, and the Royal Family was a prime target. Before Bond and I could contemplate our next move, two detectives arrived, followed by the Sergeant of the Guard and four Guardsmen. They sprang into action doing a search—nothing was found.

As for Bond and myself? We soon found ourselves in close arrest!

In the Guardroom the next day, we stood before the Commanding Officer, who read us the charges—it felt like a scene from a movie. I was amazed to find myself being charged, especially since I hadn't even fired any shots! But being the senior soldier made me responsible for everything that occurred on my post. I was confined to barracks for seven days and told to pay for the five bullets fired.

Later, we discovered that one of the statues on the lawn had been hit at least twice, proving that Bond had indeed been a good shot, albeit not necessarily at the right target! After this debacle, we spent four hours on guard duty—talk about the consequences of a mistimed shot!

Wellington Barracks

It was around early 1940 when I found myself stationed at Kempton Racecourse, but that was only for a few weeks before we migrated to Wellington Barracks on Birdcage Walk in London. Here, we had our fill of "Spit & Polish and Bull." Our duties included Barrack Guard, Buckingham Palace Guard, St. James's Palace Guard, and even the Bank of England, plus Fire Piquets. Arranging our schedules was always a challenge; it wasn't until after 6:00 p.m. that the orders would be posted on the notice board, leaving many a young lady heartbroken when her date failed to materialize. "C'est La Guerre!" became our battle cry.

It wasn't long before I found myself in trouble again, all thanks to my friend James Bond—yes, the same James Bond, though his life was a little less glamorous than his cinematic counterpart! One night, he whisked me, Vic, and a couple of others over to the Southwark area, informing us that he had relatives nearby. We quickly found ourselves in his local pub, living our best lives with a glorious night filled with beer and food, none of us spending a penny. Bond had a gift for singing and quickly became the life of the party.

By the time we left the pub near 11:00 p.m., our hopes of returning to the barracks before 11:30 were dashed, midnight rolled around before we finally made our way back. In true Bond fashion, he assured us he knew a sneaky way into the barracks, which turned out to mean climbing over the rear railing. Let me tell you, after a night of drinking, that was no mean feat!

Vic and I were the first to scale the railing, followed by Bond and the others. Unfortunately, James Bond's foot got stuck in the railings, leaving him dangling like a poorly hung Christmas ornament. Just then, we heard footsteps approaching, and Vic and I swiftly dodged to the back of the building, our hearts racing at the sound of the Barracks Police approaching.

Meanwhile, Bond and the others got caught and were placed under Close Arrest for "breaking into barracks" and being "absent." Vic and I, however? We somehow managed to escape without any charges—it must have been sheer luck on our part! I can't recall any further contact with James Bond after that; it was as if he had vanished into the shadows!

Guard Duty at Buckingham Palace

Guard duty at Buckingham Palace was a bit of a different animal, especially since we stood in front of the railings, often with the public behind us. It made marching your beat quite an adventure! And let me tell you, the public loved to snap photographs. While we weren't allowed to accept money for them, if someone "accidentally" tucked a coin into your pocket, well, who were we to argue?

One particular day, Vic and I were on duty; I was the right-hand sentry and technically in charge. As I gave the signal for patrol, we sloped arms with military precision. During our patrol, I scanned the area, and suddenly noticed a crowd of people staring down at the ground. Out of nowhere, a dog came racing past, howling in distress.

Just as I reached my sentry box to perform my "halt" (right turn, one pace back, and Order Arms), I spotted Vic on the ground. It turned out the pesky dog had been yapping at his heels, and when Vic did his about-turn, the dog had darted under his feet—down went Vic, and away went the dog as if it were competing in the sprint of the century! The crowd gathered around Vic, and although he relished the attention, he quickly learned that the Sergeant of the Guard wasn't nearly as applauding.

Vic found himself charged with "whilst on active service, idling on guard duty." I swear, the creative charges that poured from the irate Sergeant were worthy of a comedy sketch! A policeman explained that this particular dog had a notorious reputation for causing chaos, especially with the Horse Guards, but unfortunately, nothing could be done, as its owner was a high-ranking official.

Guarding the Railway Bridge

In addition to guarding Buckingham Palace, we also had shifts at the railway bridge in Staines, which was crucial for both goods and passenger trains. The guardroom was located in the local cricket club pavilion, a quaint little spot behind which flowed the River Thames. Due to threats from the IRA to blow up the railway bridge, we were always on high alert.

James Bond had the duty of guarding the guardroom, trotting around the pavilion on patrol, while I took position on the bridge itself—no small feat, especially given how long it stretched over the main London road. One night, around 1:00 a.m., my senses were suddenly heightened when I heard two rifle shots coming from the rear of the guardroom, followed by another shot that pierced through the still night air. Within moments, the peaceful surroundings transformed into chaos as a flurry of uniformed policemen, along with a handful of civilians, rushed to the scene. The commotion was enough to raise my heartbeat to alarming levels, as searchlights flared to life, illuminating the area as if we were in the middle of a crime drama.

It turned out to be James Bond's handiwork once more. He thought he'd heard movement in the bulrushes near the Thames and had shouted a challenge, but when no one responded, he decided to take action and—how do I say this delicately—the report of his rifle quite possibly made him look more like an overzealous hunter than the disciplined Guardsman he was supposed to be.

Before we had time to gather our thoughts or take any further action, the police arrived, following Bond's shots to what they assumed was a dire situation. In the early morning light, a dead swan was discovered tangled in the bulrushes—certainly not the intruder Bond had envisioned! Suddenly, the barracks turned back to being a bustling mix of military and police chatter, with a focus turning to the unfortunate circumstances surrounding James's choice of target.

Word spread quickly, and the implications of harming a swan were serious, involving not just our fearless friend, but a potential legal matter! A number of the old boys in the barracks joked with Bond about his newfound "hunting skills," but there was no hiding the fact that he'd likely find himself in hot water when the higher-ups got involved.

Looking back now, it was a harrowing experience, but we were just happy to have escaped without additional charges. As we saw officers plastering "Wanted" posters around the barracks for the "missing" James Bond, I couldn't help but think how comically absurd it all was.

Moving Around

Wellington Barracks in 1940 served as the holding Battalion for the Grenadier Guards. At that time, three Battalions were deployed as part of the British Army in France, and we were poised to join one of them at a moment's notice. The war in France was more of a slow jog than a sprint, with us first reserves itching to be drafted into action. Rumours suggested that, aside from occupying part of the Maginot Line, the Germans and Allies were playing an intense game of "stare-and-blink," neither side daring to make the first move.

Since the Maginot Line didn't extend into Belgium, the powers that be decided to build an extension along the border called the Gort Line. However, early in May 1940, the Germans made their bold move, invading Belgium, and suddenly the game changed. The Guards Brigades—1st and 7th—found themselves in a rear guard action right through Belgium.

One evening, orders were posted that the next day, thirty of us would parade in full kit, including our kit bags. The names were listed alphabetically and, as fate would have it, ended at "G." This omission meant that Bill Yates was unceremoniously left off the list. As we paraded, climbed into transport, and sped off, I found myself among a group of Guardsmen heading for France, wondering if Bill was sitting back at the barracks, nursing a pint, while we were off to war!

Once we landed somewhere near Boulogne, the confusion set in. Nobody seemed to know where we were supposed to report, as the Battalions had already shifted into Belgium and the French Army stood between us and them. It felt like a scene out of a slapstick comedy—like "Fred Karno's Setup," with everyone wandering around in chaos! Eventually, we banded together with another group of reinforcements, all of us scrambling to find the elusive 1st or 7th Division. Spoiler alert: we failed. Eventually, we ended up back on a boat headed for England and Wellington Barracks. By this point, Bill Yates had been drafted to France; little did I know it would be ages before I'd see him again.

Not long after our return, we linked up with the 3rd Battalion near Wakefield. We didn't get to enjoy paradise for long, though, as we soon found ourselves relocated to a quaint little village called North Thoresby, halfway between Louth and Grimsby. Life there meant enduring "stand-to" duties at the crack of dawn and again before dusk—prime times recognized for a German invasion. I can tell you, the tension was real! We had our fair share of scares; one time, it felt like the invasion was surely "on"—and we stood to all night, adrenaline pumping and hearts racing. Thank goodness nothing happened!

We just simply couldn't have stopped the German Army if they really decided to roll through; what I mean by "we" is "The British Army." We lacked sufficient manpower, the right armour, and enough guns, not to mention the fact that we were woefully short on fighter planes.

Looking back on those days, I can't help but chuckle at the absurdity of it all. Here we were, a ragtag group of young men thrust into the throes of war, trying to maintain a brave face even as we feared we'd have to borrow a pint of courage from the nearest pub just to get through the day!

Hats Off

Sandal was a pretty little village in Yorkshire—at least it was to the members of the 3rd Battalion Grenadier Guards. In June 1940, we had survived the chaos of Dunkirk and fought a long, defensive battle against the German Army. Our mission was clear: hold them off as long as possible to allow the British Army to evacuate as many men as they could and regroup back in England. Unfortunately, our battalion suffered heavy casualties and, as fate would have it, it was impossible to gather everyone on the same ship. It took a while to get all the survivors back to the battalion.

When we finally arrived in Sandal, we lined up on the village green, excitement buzzing in the air. A group of local folk, mostly women, walked down our line. Each woman would say a number, corresponding to how many Guardsmen she was assigned to take home. Before we knew it, we were off, escorting our designated lady to her house. I mean, can you imagine? The entire battalion was crashing at civilians' homes, and we were on full board—it was absolutely fantastic!

Vic and I ended up sharing a double room with three local blokes who worked down the coal pit, all of whom were from Ireland. After stashing our kits, we freshened up and made our way down for our meal. We sat at a lovely large dining table, with a dinner plate and cutlery for each of us. In the center of the table sat a generous plate of Yorkshire puddings along with a jug of gravy. We sat there for ages, wondering when the rest of the meal would make its grand entrance. Just as Vic was about to investigate, our landlady walked in, stared us down, then fixed her gaze on the Yorkshire puddings.

"Don't you like Yorkshire puddings?" she asked, looking genuinely concerned.

"Oh yes, I love them!" I stammered, trying to sound enthusiastic while also puzzling over the right way to eat them.

"Well, what's wrong with my pudding?" she pressed, tilting her head.

"Nothing, we're just waiting for the meat and veg!" I replied, giving a nervous chuckle. It took a moment, but the realization dawned on her: we had never experienced Yorkshire pudding in the traditional way! The plate of puddings was whisked away and replaced with a hearty serving of meat, vegetables, and that delicious gravy. That day, Vic and I officially had our first Yorkshire dinner—it was fabulous!

That evening, we sat together at the table, basking in the warmth of good food, laughter, and the camaraderie of our fellow soldiers. Little did we know, though, that the next morning would bring a fresh set of adventures.

We woke early to a lovely breakfast, and as we left the table, we heard the bugle call summoning us to assemble. We made our way to the village green—the only area we knew—and found ourselves forming a line in the shape of the letter U. A mixed group arrived, including officers, policemen, male civilians, and two rather concerned women.

As we stood at attention, the two ladies began to walk down the line, scrutinizing each Guardsman with intent. I felt a pang of sympathy for them as they appeared tired and worried. They walked the whole rank, and when they turned back, I overheard one of them lament, "We can't identify them; they all look alike!"

We were oblivious to the reason for this peculiar identification parade until the truth came tumbling out later. These two married ladies had met two Guardsmen the previous evening, while their husbands were working down the coal mine. They claimed those Guardsmen had assaulted them and were now on the lookout for their perpetrators.

Naturally, as the global champions of military fashion, our matching uniforms left them scratching their heads in confusion. To make things clearer, the Drill Sergeant suggested we remove our hats, thinking it would help narrow it down. There was a moment of silence before one of the ladies remarked, "But they didn't take their hats off anyway!"

Who those misbehaving Guardsmen were remained a mystery, and honestly, I had my doubts about the ladies' claims. Within days, we left Sandal and were reassigned to Coastal Defence operating from the town of Louth

My Pen Friend, Scotland 1941-1942

In early 1940, we left Lincolnshire bewildered. For the last two weeks, we had been on 48 hours "notice to move". Dressed in our khaki uniforms and sporting Pith helmets, it was obvious we weren't headed for the North Pole, but exactly where were we going?

It was after midnight when the troop train pulled out of the station. Having donned our khaki attire, I assumed we would be sailing from either Liverpool or Birkenhead. I told my mother to expect visitors—little did I know she would go all out decorating the house in anticipation! On the train, we travelled in every direction; North, South, East, and West. Due to war-time precautions, train stations had dispensed with their name plates, leaving us utterly clueless about our destination.

After an eternity, we finally pulled into a station around 7:30 in the morning. The whole battalion formed up behind our Drums and Fife Band and marched onwards, even though none of us knew where we were!

We paraded through a housing estate to the tune of "The Return of the Grenadiers," and arrived in Pollokshaws, on the outskirts of south Glasgow. Children of all shapes and sizes came running to greet us, all squeals and smiles. Unfortunately, the parents didn't share the same enthusiasm, their expressions more akin to a stern "Who let the dogs out?"

We had not exactly anticipated ending up in Scotland, and our first thought was "Why?" The camp was decent, a transit camp, so we assumed we would be heading overseas soon—at least we hoped, because we could really use a change in scenery!

Now, it so happened that I had become pen friends with a lovely young lady in Glasgow. My friend Vic was quite the ladies' man, charming his way through life like he was auditioning for a romantic comedy. I was eternally in his shadow; this was my chance to finally shine! We had a day pass, and off we went to Glasgow. The tram from Pollokshaws conveniently ran straight to Partick, where my pen friend Connie lived.

Some of the 3rd battalion Grenadier Guards 1942 in training in Scotland I am 6th from right no hat

When we arrived in Partick, I must admit I was slightly underwhelmed by the appearance of the area. Even at lunchtime, we spotted a few drunks loitering about—surely a sign that we were in "the good part" of town! After a bit of searching, we found the address, but my heart sank as we approached. The houses were all tenements, and at the entrance to our block stood a group of women chatting away, blocking our path. We couldn't grasp much of what they were saying—we were just focused on squeezing past them—so they found our predicament rather amusing.

After what felt like ages climbing the stairs (and avoiding the odour wafting from the communal toilet on each landing), we reached Connie's door. Vic knocked, and I swear I could have killed him for doing so! The door cracked open by only a few inches, revealing a gaunt woman who looked like she'd just come from a horror film audition. After a confusing exchange of pleasantries, a girl about eighteen appeared—almost dressed, though it was clear she had only just rolled out of bed.

She invited us in, and let me tell you: "What a dump!" The living room was scattered with clutter, and you could hardly see the fireplace for all the, well, chaos! Connie was at work and wouldn't be back until late. Apparently, her husband had walked out, and her mom was having a rough time coping with it all. I never did get to meet my lovely pen friend Connie, much to Vic's amusement—he never let me forget about my "lady friend" in Glasgow.

Our anticipated, heroic raid on a German-held island was cancelled and we were relocated to Castle Douglas. We became part of a special Brigade, trained to invade strategic areas that were now in German hands, mainly to keep the enemy on their toes and, ideally, bring back prisoners and materials. There were at least six proposed raids, but thankfully, all of them were cancelled. It's important to note that during 1940-41, we had an army in Egypt, another in India, and various units scattered around other countries.

Our time in Castle Douglas was quite pleasant. The next town over was Dalbeattie, home to an ammunition factory, where many girls worked in a shift system. In fact, there were often more girls than men to be found! Occasionally, young men would bid a heartfelt "cheerio" to one girlfriend at the train station, only for the girls to welcome another back off the return train. You can imagine the confusion; it was nearly enough to give a young man whiplash trying to keep track of who was dating who!

We spent much of our time in cross-country training, especially in the frosty terrains north of Inveraray. Winter had blanketed the mountains with pristine snow, creating breath-taking views, but we frequently ended up spending three or four nights out there, bracing against the severe cold. That said nothing quite matched the thrill of roughing it in the great outdoors, even though the biting chill that made every night an exercise in endurance!

The Fight with the Cold

Life at camp came with its own camaraderie and a fair amount of adventure. Our meals were simple, often consisting of rather bland rations, but we made the best of it with our improvised cooking skills. However, our limited culinary know-how led to some amusing mishaps. During one lunchtime, I attempted to make what I confidently labelled "World's Best Army Stew." After a thorough inspection of our meagre supplies, the result was more of a concoction based on bully beef and crackers. My fellow soldiers were polite enough to try it, but the looks on their faces suggested they were unsure at what the cook had actually meant to create!

One memorable summer day, while trekking across the hills, we stumbled upon a group of sheep. In a moment of youthful bravado, I decided it would be a good idea to try and herd them—which turned out to be more comical than productive. Picture a bunch of soldiers donning khaki uniforms and trying to corral unsuspecting sheep while the sheep formed a deliberate union against us. They slipped and dodged as we shouted, "Come by you woolly fools!" I still chuckle imagining the sheer bewilderment on their faces.

A Friend in High Places

In those years, we also learned the value of friendships and bonds that deepened through shared experiences. I was befriended by an older fellow named Harry, who had joined the army later. Harry had this impressive ability to spin tales of his escapades prior to joining up, often featuring improbable characters and hair-raising plots. We would sit around the fire, listening to his riveting stories, most of which we could only assume were exaggerated to some degree—just like Bond's legendary conquests back in London!

One day, while waiting for our rations, Harry suddenly declared, "When I get out of here, I'm going to become a world-famous chef!" Naturally, we all laughed, imagining him surrounded by glamorous diners, wielding pots and pans instead of rifles. "First dish on the menu?" I asked. "Sheep stew!" he replied with a straight face.

Tunisia 1942-1943

From Castle Douglas, we were suddenly alerted to prepare for an invasion raid on Calais, aimed at capturing some critical equipment that warned the Germans about our bombers. We packed our bags and moved down to the Isle of Wight, ready to hop the Channel at a moment's notice. But as fate would have it, poor weather due to wind and tide forced a sudden cancellation of our plans. Instead, we found ourselves back in Scotland, pulling into Perth just in time for some rather grand military inspection by the King. It should have been a sign that our time in Scotland had come to an end.

H.M. The King inspects the 3rd Battalion at Perth. Summer, 1942.
Officers (L. to R.): Capt. H. W. O. Bradley, Brig. F. A. V. Copland-Griffiths, Lt.-Col. A. G. W. Heber-Percy, Capt. K. E. M.

Soon after the inspection, we boarded the HMT Leopoldville with a destination still shrouded in mystery. I learned later that Leopoldville was sunk Dec 24 1944 by a U-Boat near Cherbourg with 750 US Soldiers "There but for the grace of God"

Would we be celebrating Christmas in Egypt, India, or Burma? We'd trained for invasion for the last eighteen months, but little did we know that our journey would lead us to Algeria instead. Eventually, we

94

learned that we were to land at Bone, a port on the border of Algeria and Tunisia, to seize control of the port and the airport.

But just when we thought we were in for action, the attack was called off at the last minute due to a lack of ships and backup. We ended up landing in Algiers during an air raid, forming up while lugging our packs and dealing with the chaos. After marching for ten gruelling miles, we settled in an open field on the outskirts of a town called Maison-Carrée (now called El Harrach). Our presence was urgently needed at the front in Tunisia, but with no transport available, the reality soon hit us, 500 miles to the front felt like an eternity away!

For the next two weeks, we marched and trained while living off the land as best we could. We even had the pleasure of calling on local French farmers, who, in a generous spirit, allowed us to take as many oranges as we could carry for a small fee. Honestly, it had been ages since we had seen an orange; our latrines were extremely busy, and a number of guardsmen ended up feeling quite ill!

Eventually, trucks became available, and off we went to join the 2nd Hampshire Battalion, which had moved ahead of us. The situation in Tunisia was getting serious. The Germans were deploying troops into Tunis by both air and sea, and we were needed to help defend the line. We took over a segment running from Bone through to Bou Arada. Our journey began on December 4, 1942, and the following day we heard the tragic news that the 2nd Hampshires had nearly been wiped out at Tebourba, about 15 miles from Tunis. They had been outmatched by the Germans, who had the upper hand with their tanks, forcing the Hampshires to withdraw—only three officers and 170 men remained.

By December 7, we found ourselves stationed just outside Beja, anticipating a German attack, so we quickly took up defensive positions. Unfortunately, it rained heavily day and night, and the makeshift shelter we had set up quickly became a fast-flowing river. Tough conditions, we were wet, cold, and hungry, cursing the rain, little did we realize that our soggy world had indirectly helped us—the German tanks were stuck in the mud and unable to advance!

When the German push finally cooled down, we were rushed to Medez-el Bab, a market town critical to the defence of Tunisia. The River Medjerda ran deep and fast, and currently, the bridge over it was damaged from shelling. Thankfully, the Royal Engineers worked tirelessly to keep that bridge open. We found defensive positions on a hillside that soon became known as "Grenadier Hill."

Our first encounter with the enemy took place on December 10, and let me tell you, it was no picnic. There were about six German tanks firing at us, and we fired back with everything we had—not so much for actual combat effectiveness, but more to give the Germans the false impression that we were a massive force. Our first casualty was Lieutenant De-Rougemont from the Mortar Platoon; sadly, he was hit by shrapnel and died in the hospital the next day.

On Christmas Day, we still found ourselves on Grenadier Hill, and as we listened to reports of the battle for Longstop Hill—a critical mountain overlooking the road to Tunis—we couldn't help but feel an odd mix of pride and melancholy. The Coldstream Guards successfully pushed the Germans off Longstop, but the Americans later took over on Christmas Eve, only to be ordered back when the Germans launched a powerful counterattack. Our Christmas dinner consisted of whatever rations we had on hand, likely from a tin, Merry Christmas

Shortly after, we were relieved and withdrew for a much-needed hot shower, a change of clothing, and a brief respite from the battlefield. But it wasn't long before we were back at Medez, now assigned to guard the area around the railway station. No. 2 Company was spread out in the woods jutting into the plain, providing cover for the station. The river was in full flow, thanks to what felt like weeks of non-stop rain.

Every morning, we adhered to our routine of "Stand To" before dawn—a standard precautionary measure against a potential attack. It was also common for the enemy to send over a few mortars and shells to keep us on our toes. On one such morning, however, things remained strangely quiet. Later that day, we spotted a German patrol making its way toward the station.

"Hold Your Fire," was the command given—so we allowed them to reach the bridge over the river. Wanting to avoid any unnecessary confrontation, we watched as two scouts led the way, casually spreading out along the river. Just when we thought it was all going smoothly, an American GI, armed with a rather heavy rifle, couldn't resist taking a shot at the leading scout. The loud crack of his rifle sent us all ducking for cover as the chaos ensued, and the seemingly calm scene exploded into mayhem!

Our Bren gunner, seeing the German patrol in his sights, opened fire, and, like something out of a comic book, a white flag fluttered in the air—whether it was from surrender or sheer confusion, we didn't care. We quickly rounded up the lot of them! There were about six wounded Germans, and one officer who was in dire straits with several bullets lodged in him. I did what I could to help him, realizing he was only a young man caught up in a terrible situation. He told me that they thought the station was deserted, which was why they had approached so casually. I knew in my gut he probably wouldn't survive his injuries, and that grim reality weighed heavily on me.

Our time defending Medez was a gruelling introduction to infantry tactics in rough terrain, especially under the persistent artillery and mortar fire from the well-trained German troops. The mountains were steep with numerous crags, providing perfect cover for the enemy and making any assault an uphill battle—quite literally!

As we endeavoured to break through the German defences, they kept us busy by attacking our weaker points to the south. The ground in the north proved unsuitable for tank warfare, as the Germans had bigger, more powerful machines than our Crusaders. The Guards Brigade shifted focus to becoming mobile infantry, a move that would allow us to support the tanks as they rolled through.

We were ordered to join forces with the 1st Parachute Battalion (Paratroopers) and the French Foreign Legion to reclaim the hills guarding a pass to Robaa. This position held strategic significance as the Germans threatened to advance through the valley between Pont du

Fahs and Bou Arada, which could split our forces in two and pave the way for their armour—the 10th Panzer Division—to break through.

We rushed to join the others and arrived just as the sun dipped below the horizon. It was decided that we would launch our attack the next day, February 5, 1943. Upon our arrival, we discovered that the Paras and Foreign Legion had already taken the objective of Djebel Mansour. Naturally, this tipped off the Germans, who were now fully prepared for our approach.

True to form, our grand strategy turned into a complete cock-up. The Foreign Legion, characteristically stubborn, insisted on taking orders only from Algiers, while the Parachute Battalion received different orders from us, resulting in three separate tactical efforts that didn't meet up at all.

At midday, we found ourselves on the start line. We advanced up the hill in open order, moving easily through the trees and bushes. But as we broke into the open about two-thirds of the way up, the Germans—clearly ready and waiting for us—opened fire with machine guns and grenades. I remember thinking, "This isn't what I signed up for!"

We suffered several casualties and severe injuries in that initial skirmish, with at least six men killed and numerous others wounded. In the chaos, it was impossible to stand straight; we had to crawl along as low to the ground as possible, dragging the more seriously wounded down the hill with us. We had captured two German prisoners, and I instructed them to carry one of our wounded while I organized the walking wounded to follow. To my surprise, the Germans were quick to comply, showing that even in times of war, a little co-operation can go a long way—though I'd bet their motives were mostly self-preservation!

Among those we carried was Sergeant Lou Druet, a close friend of ours. He had suffered severe injuries from a burst of machine gun fire that had torn across his back and spine. I spoke to the Company Sergeant Major and told him that I would have to carry Lou out. The Sergeant Major informed me that there would be no further attacks until morning; No. 3 Company was on their way through to support us.

Lou was a big chap, easily over 6 feet tall and weighing around 13 stone. We fashioned a makeshift stretcher and carefully placed him onto it, but the journey to the clearing station was laborious; it felt like we were dragging a boulder rather than a human being. We were exhausted, but we pressed on, determined to get Lou the medical attention he desperately needed.

When we finally reached our Rear Company HQ, it was about 4:00 a.m. We decided to wait until daylight; not knowing the whereabouts of my Company was nerve-wracking enough! Just as the sun began to rise, Bill Butler, the Company Runner, came rushing over. He brought disheartening news: a mortar shell had exploded near our Company Sergeant Major, leaving him badly wounded. We quickly raced down to his aid.

CSM Herbert had received a significant injury to the top of his leg, and he was unconscious. He was bleeding heavily, and without a stretcher in sight, I quickly told Wally Kershaw to dress the wound and applied a tourniquet. Our priority was to get him to a field dressing post. Carrying an injured man in these conditions was challenging and arduous, especially considering that most of the Guards weighed well over 12 stone and we were under fire.

As we made our way, our company began to pass us; it was complete havoc. Mortar shells were falling ahead of us, and there we were, trying to maintain some semblance of order and calm while evacuating our CSM. The gully was not wide enough for my little group, and we had no choice but to stick to the path.

It didn't take long for CSM Herbert to become eerily quiet, and when we checked his pulse and breathing, we realized he was dead. One of our company officers approached, and after I explained our situation and our decision to carry him out, he advised us that our services would be more valuable elsewhere. We were to leave the CSM and tend to the casualties further down the line.

As we began our withdrawal, tragedy struck again. One of my stretcher-bearers, Wally Kershaw, was wounded; he took shrapnel to the chest. I was occupied helping another lad and didn't know Wally had been hit until we reached our safe zone. Wally was a brave chap and, coincidentally, hailed from my hometown of Birkenhead, just like my other stretcher bearer, Tom Higginson. We were a tight-knit team, but the war was about to test our bonds more than we could have ever anticipated.

After pulling back about a mile from the front, our battalion had suffered around 100 casualties—officers and men killed or wounded. Thankfully, we found ourselves well behind the frontline, in a territory where slit trenches had already been dug—almost one for each of us! We set about brewing up some tea and opened our Compo Boxes, which contained enough food for 100, yet only about 60 or 70 of us were left.

Because everything was in tins, once you popped one open, you had to use it all, which quickly became a culinary conundrum considering our varied tastes. Picture a group of soldiers negotiating over a can of baked beans—honestly, it was farcical.

The following morning, Major Bolitho, our Company Commander, summoned me to discuss the battle and our casualties. We settled on a hillside, and I recounted my version of events, highlighting the bravery of my comrades Wally and Tom. After I finished, he said, "Well done; tell your chaps that all the wounded have been accounted for." Confused, I wondered why I had been asked to give this account—the Medical Officer was usually in charge of that sort of thing!

Months later, I was called to attend the "Commanding Officer's Memoranda." Marching in, I was a mix of nerves and curiosity as the CO read out everything that had occurred at Djebel Allilga. To my surprise, he extended his hand to shake mine, awarded me the Distinguished Conduct Medal (DCM)—one of the highest honours in the British Army!

OUR WAR HEROES

It was in Tunisia, just before the total defeat of the enemy, when our heroic forces were driving on to victory. The Grenadier Guards were well to the fore as they have been in so many past campaigns the world over, and were attacking the strong enemy position at Alliliga Hill, near Bou Arada. The ground was rocky and precipitous with almost sheer slopes and dotted with thick scrub and brush. Heavy enemy fire took deadly toll of the Guardsmen, and Lance-Cpl. John Byrne and three stretcher-bearers toiled hard, under incessant fire, to evacuate the wounded.

For twenty four hours, day and night, they worked without a break, and all the time were deliberately sniped by the enemy. Across "impossible country"—as the official record puts it—they carried the wounded, and how hard their task was you will realise when you hear that it took Lance-Cpl. Byrne and another man nine hours to carry a wounded sergeant two miles, including the time when, on the way, he stopped and attended six other wounded men. In all, Lance-Cpl. Byrne and his helpers successfully evacuated thirty wounded men, displaying—again to quote the official record—"amazing stamina." For his unflinching devotion to his wounded comrades, Lance-Cpl. Byrne was awarded the D.C.M.

DISTINGUISHED CONDUCT MEDAL

2616748 Lance Corporal John BYRNE
3rd Bn Grenadier Guards

On Thursday 4 February 1943 at about 1500 hours, the Coy of the A/N L/Cpl attacked ALLILIGA HILL near BOU ARADA. For the next 24 hours L/Cpl BYRNE and his three Company Stretcher Bearers worked without a break; the conditions under which they laboured were appalling; the ground was of a rocky, precipitious nature, with almost vertical slopes, and interspersed with thick scrub and bushes; throughout the 24 hours L/Cpl BYRNE and his bearers were subjected to heavy mortar fire, machine gun fire and, whilst tending the wounded, deliberate sniping; in no way did this deter L/Cpl BYRNE from organising and encouraging his bearers in a calm continuance of the many and great tasks which faced them that afternoon and night. As one example only of what he did during the action, I would cite the case of a L/Sgt whom he and another bearer carried for 2 miles over this difficult country, from 1600 hours to 0100 hours, in order to bring him eventually to an advanced RAP, dressing and attending six wounded men en route. Having done this he at once returned to his company, made an improvised stretcher with rifles, and helped carry his CSM, who ultimately died, for a mile, over what could practically be called impossible going.

According to all reports the powers of stamina as displayed by L/Cpl BYRNE during the action were amazing, his example of devotion to duty, a very fine one, and the encouragement and leadership he gave to those working under him, quite outstanding. One of his stretcher bearers, incidentally, became a casualty during the night; as a result of L/Cpl BYRNE's work during the engagement, some thirty casualties were tended, under fire, successfully evacuated.

Curious, I inquired whether Kershaw and Higginson had also received the award, only to discover they had not. A wave of guilt washed over me, prompting me to write to our local Birkenhead newspaper to share the story and highlight the bravery of Wally and Tom. To my disappointment, the Birkenhead News never responded. I often wonder if my letter even made it past the censors—perhaps they deemed it too sensitive for public consumption!

On the bright side, our minor defeat was a blessing in disguise; the Germans decided to abandon their plans to take Robaa but were forced to keep troops stationed there—an expense they could ill afford. In the meantime, we took up defensive positions in Robaa just in case they decided to come charging back.

When the fighting around Medez-el-Bab finally died down, we were given a well-deserved break. The mobile bath unit arrived, and let me tell you, nothing could beat that feeling of a hot shower, a fresh set of underwear, and a hot meal—a true luxury amid the chaos! The CSM gathered us around and announced that we would have at least a week off. Even better, a small group would be heading to Philippeville for a short break—I was among the lucky crew!

We packed up with no time wasted, collected some money, and off we went—a very happy bunch indeed! Our billet was a spacious room above a cinema; the beds were pallet beds filled with straw, which felt like absolute bliss after weeks of sleeping in a muddy hole dug into a hillside!

While there, I noticed a hairdressing salon across from our billet. Curious, I wandered in. The manager greeted me in his less-than-fluent English, and I responded in my dreadful French. It turned out he had served in the French Navy, and he welcomed us with open arms, genuinely hoping we'd help rattle the Germans. When I mentioned we'd just come from Medez-el-Bab, the ladies in the salon erupted in applause and kind remarks.

When I exited the salon, I couldn't shake the feeling that I looked and smelt like a complete pansy. I ended up with a reputation that I could have done without!

Later on, we decided to split into small groups to explore the town further. I was in a group of four as we sauntered around the main square until we discovered a café called "Le Chat Noir," which sported a rather extensive bar. We plopped ourselves down at one end, utterly clueless about what to order. Of course, beer was off the menu, so we ended up with bottles of wine—why not indulge, right?

At the far end of the bar, I spotted Tommy Francis, my neighbour from Birkenhead. We recognized each other immediately, and as it happened, Tommy was with the Royal Engineers. Most of the chaps he hung out with were from our area too, which made for an excellent reunion.

We migrated to their billets, situated in a large warehouse. The laughter we generated was loud enough to disturb the rest of the company, and it wasn't long before the MPs arrived to calm us down and send us back to our billets.

When I woke up the next morning, I felt dreadful, like I had been hit by a truck. I was worried I might be sick. After sitting for what felt like ages on the steps of our billet, I decided to make my way to the hairdressing salon across the road. Jean, the manager, took me by the arm and guided me to a chair squeezed between two ladies. The place was bustling, and I was pretty sure I was the only guy in the room.

As Jean chatted away, I understood very little of what he said, but I made an effort to explain my previous night at "Le Chat Noir." He kept the conversation lively, throwing in words that went over my head. When he asked if I had been drinking, I replied in my best French, "Oui, beau zig-zig." To my surprise, everyone laughed. Then, when he asked how many I had had, I boldly said, "cinq fois." This only drew more laughter from the ladies, and I couldn't quite grasp why.

At that moment, an officer in the US Army stood up from the far end of the room and approached me with a knowing smile. He said, "You've got your zig-zigs and your zig-zags mixed up, Corporal." I was taken aback, realizing I had accidentally claimed to have had quite a different experience that night. I hurriedly wiped the soap off my face and made my way out, receiving applause from the ladies on my way out. Oh la la!

As for the war, things weren't any less perplexing. I wasn't entirely sure if the Germans aimed to pin down Allied forces at Robaa and Medez-El-Bab or if they simply wanted to create chaos. With the Guards Brigade being the only mobile troops available, we rushed from one challenge to another. Surprisingly, our casualties were light. The Germans had shifted their focus further south, attacking between Sbiba and Kasserine, having already taken Faid, Sbeitla, and Gafsa.

Things escalated quickly when we learned that the Germans had overrun the Americans and seized control of the Kasserine Pass. My company (No. 2 company) was ordered to approach along the ridge of hills, while No. 1 comp navigated the slopes and No. 4 comp moved through the valley. Our Major, John Nelson, had been wounded, and his driver was killed when they hit a mine. We faced numerous casualties as we advanced to the opening of the pass, only to find six American soldiers who had tragically lost their lives.

I organized their burial, took down their names and numbers, and said a prayer as we laid them to rest. Why the Germans decided to withdraw, I can't say—perhaps Rommel thought he had created a significant breach in the Allies' defences, and he knew the 8th Army was making headway, pushing the Germans and Italians through Libya and into Tunisia.

By this point, the 3rd Battalion Grenadier Guards had earned the nickname "The Plumbers," as we were frequently called upon to fill gaps in the Allied line. We barely had time to assess the Kasserine Pass before we were on the move again, this time to El-Aroussa. Upon arrival, we found that the enemy had pulled back, leaving behind a trove of equipment. Occasionally, that meant moving a dead German to secure the items we needed. Alongside the Coldstream Guards, we rushed around to prevent any breakthroughs. The Germans found themselves caught in a difficult position but were not about to give up easily.

Eventually, we found ourselves back defending Medez-El-Bab, occupying Grenadier Hill and "The Cave," which was Battalion HQ.

On March 22, 1943 (the day after my 23rd birthday), we pulled out of Medez and assembled around Sidi-Youssef. As was becoming our custom, No. 2 comp was camped on the outskirts of town—I never actually saw Sidi-Youssef. By this time, we had transformed into the motorized infantry of the 6th Armoured Division, along with the Coldstream and Welsh Guards (the 1st ever Guards Brigade). We had to adapt to a new training routine to work closely with the tanks. The armour consisted of the 17th/21st Lancers, 16th/ 5th Lancers, and Derbyshire Yeomanry.

The tanks had been updated to Shermans, which, while not as formidable as the German Tiger, at least had better speed and firepower compared to our Valentines. However, the Shermans had their own weaknesses, as they could easily catch fire. We were gearing up for what would be the final battle for Tunis, with the 8th Army poised to break through "The Mareth Line" and into Tunisia in the coming weeks.

The Mareth Line and operations in 1943

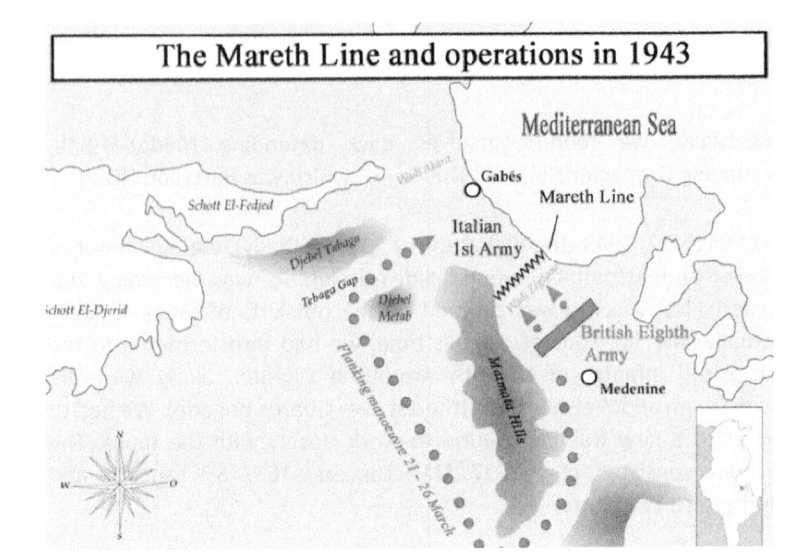

The Germans' tactics became clear: by keeping the 1st Army, the French, and the Americans busy, the retreating Germans could make Tunis and Cap-Bon their own version of Dunkirk. Their goal was to evacuate as many troops as possible and ship them over to Italy. The 6th Armoured Division was now ready to put General Alexander's plan into action. They would attack through Fondouk, breaking out of the mountains and onto the plains. The British 128th Brigade and the American 34th Division were set to make the initial attack, aimed at forcing a breakthrough for the tanks of the 6th Armoured Division to cut off the German retreat.

The British 128th Brigade executed a brilliant attack and successfully captured their objectives. Unfortunately, the American attack didn't go as planned, so the 3rd Battalion Welsh Guards were sent in to secure the high ground of Djebel-El-Rhorab. This was their first attack, and it was quite successful—the tanks of the British 6th Armoured Division broke through onto the plain, while the Grenadiers stood by in reserve. We followed the advance up to Kairourah, joining up with the 8th Army led by Montgomery. No. 2 comp could see Kairourah in the distance, gleaming white and beautiful, but we didn't get the chance to step foot in that lovely city. The 8th Army claimed priority and pressed on toward

Sousse. Now with the tanks finding ideal conditions for their warfare, the infantry struggled to keep pace.

The 6th Armoured Division pulled out and formed up just outside Medez-El-Bab, preparing for the final push to capture Tunis and stop the Germans from taking refuge in the mountainous region of Cap-Bon. In our sector south of Medez-El-Bab, the 5th and 6th Battalions were alongside every unit of the Guards Brigade. For the first time, the Grenadiers, Coldstream, Scots, Irish, and Welsh were all fighting together. Once the final push began, each battalion took on their tasks, with my 3rd Battalion held in reserve. The effort was so successful that we found it tough to keep up!

As we reached the outskirts of Tunis, we got orders to head to Hammam-Lif and seal off Cap-Bon. There were still ten German divisions and five Italian divisions aggressively fighting. In our drive to Tunis, we had effectively split the German forces in two. Meanwhile, the 6th Armoured Division faced enemy forces on both the northern and southern flanks, while the 7th Armoured Division advanced on our southern side.

Upon entering Hammam-Lif, we surrounded the Bey's Palace, detained him, and set mounted guards at the gate. No. 2 company was positioned on the outskirts of the town when the Germans began firing mortars, resulting in several civilian casualties. We did our best to assist them; an ambulance arrived, and I organized the wounded. One incident stuck with me: an Arab family had a woman injured by shrapnel in her upper leg, but her husband refused to let me dress the wound. He wanted all his family in the ambulance with her. I tried to explain, but it took a French officer telling him "Allez!" to finally convince him. I have no idea what happened to the woman after that. When I returned to my Company's area, they had moved on! Eventually, I encountered two Military Policemen, who informed me that No. 2 comp had gone into Cap-Bon. The Germans were still firing mortars from the mountains, and since it was getting late, the Policemen advised me to stay in town for the night; they'd arrange for me to join my company in the morning.

The next day, when I was taken up into the mountains, I met my Company coming back down. It turned out the Germans had surrendered, and I had spent a sleepless night for nothing. The Bey, who had one hundred wives, had been taken away, prompting us to draw lots for his wives. I drew number 38—what she looked like? I have no idea, as we moved on quickly.

The tanks were far ahead of us, and we had trouble managing the prisoners and sending them back to Hammam-Lif. We ended up on the lower slopes of the mountains on our way to Bouficha. General von Arnim of the German Army had been captured, along with General Graf von Sponeck of the 90th Light Division. In Bouficha, he expressed that it was a "privilege to surrender to the Grenadier Guards, the finest troops in the British Army." Nice of him! It was surprising to see battalions of German troops marching into captivity, looking almost like they were on a victory parade—no disgruntled faces or sloppiness.

Next, we received orders to continue south and join up with the 8th Army. We moved in battle formation, with carriers leading the way and the companies following in their lorries. As we approached a wadi that was quite steep, we found the bridge had been blown, blocking our path. However, when the advance party of the 8th Army arrived, they quickly built a bridge, allowing us to cross and finally join up with them.

The following day, we left the area and returned to Hammamet to take charge of a prisoner-of-war camp and enjoy some downtime on the shores of the Mediterranean.

In Tunis, a Victory Parade was held, and four of us—Tommy Higginson, Alfie Mosely, Joe Pratt, and I—took part. We positioned ourselves at the rear of our Company, with our first-aid bags and wearing Red Cross armbands. As we marched proudly along the grand boulevard, we were greeted with loud cheers from the crowd. It felt good to know our job in Tunis was complete!

A rest camp was quickly set up in Hammam-Lif, a lovely seaside resort on the Cap-Bon peninsula not far from Tunis. I was fortunate to spend a few days there in a beautiful house. We had an Italian POW who was an excellent accordion player, and it was a pleasure to relax and listen to his music—he was quite popular among us. However, on my second day there, a tragedy unfolded. For reasons only he knew, he took a rifle, put the barrel in his mouth, and pulled the trigger. I arrived just minutes after the shot to find him dead. We never learned what drove him to such a heart breaking act.

Having captured a German paymaster and his safe full of money, along with other sources of cash, we suddenly found ourselves with lots of cash, mainly in large notes. Our camp was outside of Sousse, where we lived in small tents scattered across a large field. One afternoon, the camp Director announced that a bank in town would accept our large Franc notes, which triggered a mad scramble to make it before closing time.

You can imagine the scene: a long line of men forming outside the bank, all eager to exchange their notes. The bank manager quickly realized he didn't have enough change and limited the amount each person could exchange, which was frustrating. A 1,000 Franc note might only be worth 500 Francs to them! To make matters worse, the Military Police arrived, shutting down the bank and sending us away empty-handed.

The next morning, we were ordered to a full company parade and formed three sides of a square, with the officers taking up the fourth side. Our Company Commander informed us that our Lieutenant Colonel Herbert-Percy was returning to England, and he would present a substantial donation to the Widows' Fund and to the restoration of the Guards' Chapel, which had been destroyed by enemy bombing. This gesture helped us dispose of most of our French Francs, and some of our officers even offered to give us half of the value in the form of cheques that we could send back home. I struck a deal and sent £50 home, glad to contribute to family back there.

Our stay in the fields outside Sousse didn't last long. The 1st Guards Brigade was selected to invade the Island of Pantelleria. We were lined up and ready to head out to attack the Italian troops on the island when we received a message from the Italians. Apparently, they had run out of water and, in a bid to save lives, offered to surrender. Our landing crafts brought back the entire garrison, and our job became guarding the prisoners. It was a stroke of luck for us that we were tasked with the Pantelleria invasion instead of the plans for Sicily.

After leaving Sousse, we found ourselves in Guelma, a town on the border of Algeria and Tunisia. We had nice accommodations in an agricultural college and settled into a routine of foot and arms drills. Nearby, the local football team was quite good; their pitch was just hard ground—no grass whatsoever. Most of the players were Arabs and didn't wear boots. They were incredibly quick and had excellent ball control.

A match was organized, and for reasons that still baffle me, I was made Centre-Forward (I usually played Half-Back). Their football skills far surpassed ours, but they struggled to get past our goal. With just a few minutes left and the score at 0-0, our goalkeeper launched a long kick toward me. I was isolated, my back to their goal, with a defender right on my heels. Falling backward as the ball approached shoulder height, I kicked it over my head. Their goalkeeper had moved forward off his line, and the ball flew over him and into the goal. We won 1-0 against a team that hadn't lost a match in three years!

Our Commanding Officer arranged for some nurses from the Field Hospital to come to the college for a dance. With a good dance band, most of us were eager for the evening. As usual, some of the lads started drinking before the nurses arrived. One chap named Alfie had a bit too much and was making a fool of himself on the dance floor. Realizing he had to be removed, I joined his antics, leading him to the door and out onto the path. Just then, our Commanding Officer and several other officers escorting the nurses turned the corner and bumped right into Alfie. He was so far gone that he had no control over his balance or his tongue. In the end, Alfie and I spent the night in the Guardroom. The next morning, I "lost my stripes," but I had two of my three stripes returned the following day.

Not long after, I met a local family. The father managed the local bank and had three children, the eldest being a very pretty girl of about 13. The mother was warm and proud of her family. One day, I received word that their daughter was very ill and they couldn't find a doctor. I rushed over to the house. Given the delicate nature of the situation, it was challenging for a male to examine a young girl; she was in severe lower stomach pain and needed immediate medical attention. I suggested a hospital, which had been taken over by the British Army. I managed to get a jeep and drove her there. She underwent an appendectomy, and I became something of a local hero!

Not long after this incident, a young boy came to our tent asking for my help at his house. The language barrier made it tricky to understand the problem! I followed him to his home, where he showed me his dog in the garden. The poor thing was foaming at the mouth, shaking, and racing about. To me, it looked like rabies! I returned to my tent, took a revolver, loaded it, and headed back to the house. By now, a crowd had gathered outside. I opened the patio door slightly; the dog charged up to me, and as it grabbed the barrel of my revolver, I pulled the trigger. Just like that, we had a dead dog! I walked back to camp to cheers and applause. I felt like a hero—having saved a girl's life and taken out a mad dog! I was sorry to leave Guelma.

We departed Guelma, still uncertain of our future role. With Sicily taken and the invasion of Italy underway, there was talk that the 1st Guards Brigade might return to England to prepare for the invasion of France. Rumours ran rampant! We ended up in Constantine, where the camp was quite nice, with everyone living in Nissen huts. Although it was a pleasant walk from the outskirts of Constantine to town, I appreciated it. Upon leaving Guelma, the French family I met had given me an introduction letter for their relatives in Constantine, who welcomed me and Vic Adams into their family.

The relatives owned a jewellery shop and lived above it in spacious rooms. The family included a father, mother, two daughters aged 16 and 18 and a young son who was just three years old. There was also an aunt and her husband. The mother was quite well-known as a French radio star, so they had a wide circle of friends. Vic and I enjoyed some lovely evenings with them, although we could never quite figure out what the parties were celebrating. One occasion seemed to be in honour of the young boy—I think it might have been a circumcision ceremony, but I'm not entirely sure. The family was Jewish, which added another layer of cultural richness to our interactions.

At every gathering, Vic and I would sing "Chattanooga Choo Choo" and "The Woodpecker Song." I'm still not sure why those two songs, but they became our unofficial anthems for the evenings! Vic had a good singing voice, but mine? Well, let's just say it was more of a comical fog horn than anything to be proud of!

Meanwhile, the boxing championships were underway. I was entered as a middleweight, which meant I needed to shed 3 pounds. I was advised to visit the hot baths in the Arab quarters, and off I went. Upon entering the baths, I was shown to a cubicle and instructed to strip down—which I did, standing there in my birthday suit. Just then, a woman came in and handed me an extra-large bath towel, taking my clothes and directing me into a massive room that was this with steam. Initially, I couldn't see a thing.

Suddenly, a hand grabbed me and I was placed against a very hot wall. I sat down for some time and began to sweat profusely. Afterward, I was taken into another room that was so stifling I could barely breathe. There, a huge man began to massage my body with his feet! He stretched every joint like he was using a squeegee. All the while, there was a constant stream of hot water running through the wall into a trough, and he drenched me with buckets of this awful-smelling water. The final bucket, however, was ice-cold—and that certainly shattered any pleasure I was feeling!

After my session, I was led back to my cubicle and left to sleep it off. When I awoke, my clothes were neatly folded, and my Army boots had been polished. As I got dressed, I noticed I was walking like I'd just come from a night out—I felt like my boots weighed a ton! I don't remember much about my walk back to camp, but I did manage to make weight for my boxing matches.

I competed in three fights, ultimately losing the third bout. I was disappointed, believing I had actually won that one! But regardless of the outcome, the experience was lively and memorable, full of camaraderie and a chance to engage with local culture—something I always cherished during my time in Tunisia.

Italy

In February of 1944, nine months after our victory in Tunisia, things weren't looking great in the war in Italy. We couldn't quite understand why we were still stuck in Constantine—there were a lot of unpleasant rumours floating around. However, we finally crossed the Mediterranean on February 4th. The crossing was dreadful; the sea was angry and our ship, the Ville d'Oran, was not the sturdiest vessel in a gale. Most of the troops were seasick, but I was lucky enough to avoid that fate.

We landed in the mid-afternoon, were quickly herded onto a train, and then piled into lorries heading to a village called Cascano. After spending the night there, we marched up to the front lines the next day. The weather was cold and rainy as we progressed toward the mountains, which were topped with snow. The 46th British Division had worked hard to push through Southern Italy, managing to cross the River Carigliano, but they had suffered heavy casualties. At that point, the 1st Guards Brigade was unattached, which meant we provided much-needed relief for the weary 46th Division. They had done an excellent job and certainly deserved a break.

While the Germans had also incurred significant casualties, they had the advantage of retreating to well-prepared defences, which made their lives a bit easier than ours. We soon learned that the 1st Guards Brigade had been rushed to Italy for an attack on the town of Castleforte—a key stronghold in the defence line through Casino—but that attack was called off at the last minute. Since we were fresh troops nearby, it made sense for us to help ease the pressure on the 46th Division.

The Germans had anticipated the advance of the Allied Forces and strategically selected positions on high ground that overlooked various rivers scattered across Italy—roughly ten to twelve miles apart. To make matters worse, all these rivers were flooded due to heavy rain and an unusual thaw. Naturally, the Germans had blown up all the bridges as they retreated, making our situation even trickier. They knew the terrain well and had the range to target every inch of our line facing them. In the first three weeks after our arrival at the Italian front, the 1st Guards Brigade suffered 400 casualties, both killed and wounded, mainly from mortar fire. Fortunately, the Grenadier Guards experienced only 38 casualties; the Coldstream Guards and the Welsh Guards shared the remainder.

The mountains presented significant challenges—evacuating a wounded man on a stretcher could take six to eight hours, followed by another three to four hours to return to your position. Yet, despite the terrible weather and lack of sleep, I don't recall anyone catching a cold.

At one point, No. 2 comp was sent to assist the Coldstream Guards, who were nearly surrounded by the Germans. Captain P. Maclean led the charge, and we succeeded in pushing the enemy back. We set up on a mountain called "Monte Ornito," a strategically significant position well out front of our line. Our hold on the mountain was crucial to keeping the Germans away from our main force. We faced our fair share of mortar shells and grenades. Tragically, during the hours of darkness, we lost Captain Maclean, along with Sergeant Bob Smart and Lou Pickerill, our Company Clerk. On a brighter note, we did manage to capture a few prisoners from their nightly patrols, which boosted our morale. They complained about our precise and deadly 25lb bombs, looking young and terrified in the process.

After a stint on the mountain, we rotated out for a short rest and change of clothes before returning, this time to "Monte Cerasola." We found ourselves perched on one side of the mountain, with the Germans just on the other side—only about 20 yards apart. Our sangers (makeshift shelters) had wire netting over them to protect us from hand grenades. Behind us, the sky lit up at night from the eruptions of Mount Vesuvius. There were rumours that our intended assault on Castleforte was cancelled because the eruptions illuminated the sky, making it too easy for the Germans to see our movements.

On March 20th, we pulled out and took over the village of Calvisi, something the locals weren't too pleased about! But our needs were greater than theirs—we had mobile baths, a change of clothes, and on March 21st (my birthday), we got a day off in Naples. I went to see Vesuvius, but unfortunately, the massive mountain was hidden behind clouds of smoke and dust. We could see the wall of lava moving forward, with a strong smell of sulphur in the air. Naples itself wasn't very inviting and appeared to be struggling.

It was in Calvisi that we re-joined the 6th Armoured Division, expecting to be held in reserve while waiting for the breakthrough at Casino. We had barely settled in with the tanks when orders came in for us to join the New Zealand Division on the River Gari, located south of Casino. Shortly after that, on April 7th, we moved into Casino itself. We all believed we would soon be called upon to launch an attack to drive the elite German paratroopers out of the town and open up the route leading to Rome.

Casino

The Abbey of Monte Casino, built in 529 by St. Benedict, was never intended to be a fortress; it was a place of worship. Perched atop Monte Casino, the Abbey overlooked the town below—now called Casino—situated there to be closer to God. Throughout history, many places of worship have been built on mountains for this very reason. Casino Abbey was the first of its kind, and since St. Benedict hailed from a wealthy family, he had the means to construct it, thereby founding "The Benedictine Order." The monks there became scholars, missionaries, and teachers, respected around the world, with Casino Abbey serving as their headquarters. Over the years, the Abbey's location made it a guardian of the Liri Valley, stretching all the way from Naples to Rome.

ITALIAN CAMPAIGN 1943-45

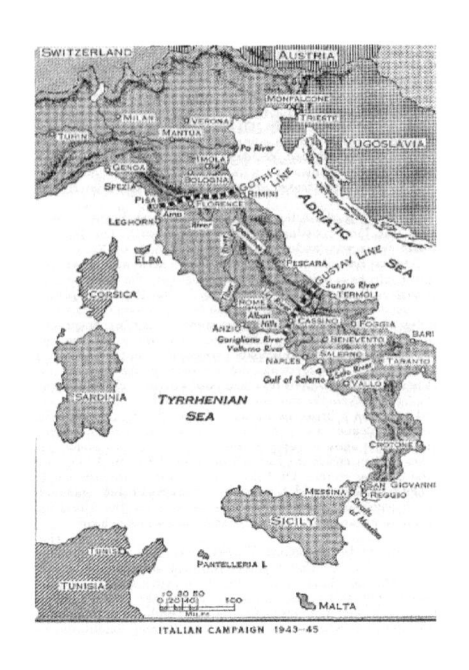

Casino Abby in ruins

116

What was left of Casino town

The Germans recognized the strategic potential of Casino and thus built a defensive line across Italy, stretching from the Adriatic to the Tyrrhenian Sea. Some of the mountains in this defensive line were among the highest in Italy, effectively interlocking their positions as you retreated north toward Rome—it was indeed a tough nut to crack!

From Monte Casino, the entire approach toward Casino Town was visible. Nothing could move without being seen. The Allies appeared to be almost overwhelmed by the defences at Casino, except for the French Division, who proposed a plan to bypass Casino via Castleforte, but that suggestion was turned down. The New Zealanders were adamant about taking Casino; how much the Anzio landings influenced the decision regarding Casino is something that remains unanswered.

At that time, there were 18 German divisions in Italy, comprising over 500,000 men. It was unfortunate for us that the Germans had chosen to build their defensive line around the Abbey, which served as a pivotal point. From a military standpoint, it made sense; however, for the Allies, it was a contentious issue. Breaking this line was critical—Route 6 through Casino was the direct path to Rome, and the Abbey was "the ever-watchful eye" for the Germans. Reports indicated that German soldiers were seen in and around the Abbey, and it had to be taken out of commission.

Every day, we cast our eyes toward Casino, knowing Route 6 was the primary route to Rome. We watched as bombers flew over Casino to target the Abbey. To say we "saw" the bombing might be an exaggeration; after the first few bombs, there wasn't much left to see— just smoke! We also noticed several bombs fell outside the intended target area. In fact, it was said that the Allies sustained more casualties from their own bombing than the Germans did! One of the Indian divisions, positioned at least nine miles away, suffered a good number of casualties during those air raids. With 500 bombers raining down bombs on Casino, we believed that every German soldier in the town would either be dead or rendered "bomb-happy" (not fit for further action).

The New Zealanders made another attempt to take the town but failed. Then the Polish forces attacked the Abbey, only to face the same fate, suffering heavy casualties in the process. Despite the bombing campaign, the damage done to the buildings and the numerous bomb craters turned Casino into a solid barrier against any kind of vehicle movement.

The Guards Brigade was pulled out of the mountains, giving us a much-needed bath, a change of clothes, and a day out in Naples. Just as we were starting to relax, we received word that Casino was our next task. The Americans had tried and failed, the New Zealanders had given it a go, and the Polish Army had also come up short. Now it was our turn, the brave lads of the Guards Brigade, on April 7th, 1944.

You can imagine our apprehension—no armour for support. Bombs and shells hadn't convinced the German Parachute Regiment to surrender, so we knew it would come down to the trusty bayonet! First things first, we had to get into Casino. The Germans had flooded the area surrounding our approach, leaving us with only one way in: Route 6. This road was perched about six feet above the fields, it was like a game of chicken, while we the Germans took pot shots.

To add to the excitement, the two bridges over the River Gari had been blown, so the Royal Engineers built us a temporary walkway. We debussed about a mile from the bridge, starting our trek from a cemetery—always a great spot to begin a life-threatening mission! We huddled behind headstones and chapels, trying to stay out of sight. The area was under shell-fire and had a stench that took your breath away. We tied sacks over our boots to muffle the sound and then set off, section by section.

The enemy had fixed their guns on Route 6, and every so often, we were greeted with bursts of machine-gun fire and the occasional mortar bomb. I found that running with my nose nearly touching the ground was not exactly the most comfortable experience. My section was almost the last to leave the cemetery, and I was relieved to note that we hadn't suffered any casualties so far. We ended up in the Crypt of the Convent, the first large building as we approached Casino. Getting into the Crypt was not difficult—you practically slid down into it!

The building had been badly damaged, with not a single wall standing. We were just happy to be out of the open—there must have been hundreds of tons of rubble above us. We had three rooms: one for the signallers, a tiny room for our officer and CSM, and a larger space for about eight of us.

Our first job was to check the food, water, ammunition, lookout posts, and the like. We had just about completed our checks when our officer asked for a report of our findings. He needed to know if everything was in order before heading back to HQ. I replied, "Sir" (in the Grenadiers, you never simply say "Yes"—it's always "Sir" or "Sergeant"). "What's behind that curtain?" he asked. I hadn't looked, so I crossed the room and peered behind the curtain. To my horror, it was the latrine—a huge biscuit tin, completely full. "Clean it out! I'll check on my return," he ordered. Well, it was evident that no one was volunteering for that delightful task.

So, I suggested we draw names to see who would do the honours. The first name out was Buck Ryan, followed by Bogey Holmes, who flatly refused. Then it was my turn. A cradle of telephone wire was placed around the biscuit tin. Realizing it was best to be above the tin for its journey up the chute, I decided to go first. After managing to get the tin safely out of the Crypt, I set off to find a good spot to dispose of the mess. I stumbled through a broken archway and was greeted by a huge bomb crater. Never in a thousand years would we be able to fill that hole!

So, I headed back to collect the tin. I figured it was best just to empty it since we would need the tin for something more important, like maybe storing cookies or something. I threw the contents into the crater—not exactly the most pleasant scent! Next, I called for water and some creosote, swished out the tin, emptied it, and placed it back behind the curtain—job well done!

In the meantime, tea had been brewed, and I sat down on my bed, ready to enjoy a nice cup when suddenly a huge commotion erupted. A figure came crashing through the blanket that covered the entrance to the Crypt. As the figure stood to their full height, I realized it was the RSM of the Coldstream Guards. He was covered in bits of paper and other unspeakable things and had a delightful aroma that reminded me of latrines! "Who threw that bucket of ****?!" he bellowed, looking quite upset. Nobody said a word, but all eyes instinctively turned toward me. "Get two men and some cleaning rags and follow me," he ordered with a commanding glare. Would you believe it, but Bogey was the first to volunteer! I'm sure he was just eager to escape the scrutiny of the RSM, or perhaps he had a secret desire to become an amateur sanitation engineer.

So, at a reasonable distance, we trailed after the RSM (who was more affectionately known as "Rotten Smelly Meat") as we navigated through the broken archway and approached the large hole. To save ourselves from stepping in something undesirable, we turned to face the hole from the opposite direction. There was a ladder protruding out of the crater, and the RSM called out, "Watch where you put your hands on the ladder!" before disappearing down it.

Following him down the ladder, we found ourselves in the Brigade HQ. The room was a chaotic mess of wireless sets, telephones, and—oh joy—was also decorated with the unfortunate remnants of our biscuit tin disaster. In the adjoining room, the officers were having a rough time as well, adorned with the contents of the biscuit tin like some sort of bizarre military fashion statement—there were more "potty" jokes being made than I'd ever thought possible.

There were a number of guardsmen already cleaning up the mess, and we quickly joined in, wiping down the wireless sets and trying not to laugh at the absurdity of it all. My Company Commander was there too, having miraculously avoided the chaos, and he wanted nothing to do with me, as if I had just entered the scene of a bad slapstick comedy.

After we finished cleaning, we returned to our part of the Crypt and settled down to enjoy a mug of tea, hoping for a little peace after the chaos. That's when I received a handwritten message—it was from the German Parachutists, congratulating me on realizing that what we thought was the Officers' Mess was nothing more than a toilet! It was a famous incident, and one of the junior officers even offered 60 cigarettes to whoever could write the best poem about it. I guess humour really is the best medicine, even in war!

As if the day hadn't been eventful enough, we soon found ourselves back in a more serious situation. Sergeant Treeby, DCM, had not returned to his platoon, prompting some concern. A search party was organized, and unfortunately, he was found dead; we had no idea how or why he had died. It was a sobering moment—the first casualty we faced in Casino. A few days later, we learned that he had been killed by a sniper's bullet.

In Casino, most of the day was spent sleeping. There was always someone on watch, and movement was rare—except for the German stretcher parties carrying wounded men toward the Abbey. They made this trip so often that it raised our suspicions, but we couldn't figure out what they were up to since their traffic only seemed to go one way.

To keep the Germans from seeing our activities, the artillery fired smoke bombs over the town. These shells exploded in the air, which meant there was a risk of being injured by falling casings. Every night, supplies came in thanks to a group called "The Porters," made up of Guardsmen from Battalion HQ. They had a tough job being our only link to the outside world. On their way back, they carried empty supplies, the wounded, and sadly, the dead, along with our mail. Remarkably, despite all the bullets and mortar fire they faced, they had no casualties! Honestly, being underground in Casino was way better than freezing on the mountainside while under fire.

After two weeks, we finally pulled out of Casino, hardly believing it. We had been tasked with driving the German 1st Parachute Regiment out of town, and every German soldier who fought there for two weeks got the Iron Cross. We returned to Calvisi for a quick "FFI" (Fit, Free from Infection) and had a change of Commanding Officer. Lieutenant Colonel Heber-Percy was promoted to Brigadier and was succeeded by Lieutenant Colonel Goshen—not exactly an upgrade!

On May 4th, 1944, we returned to Casino for what would be the final battle. This time, no one knew exactly when the "Big Push" would begin. We set up in three houses: Mary, Jane, and Helen. Company HQ was in House Mary, which had no cellar, so we were all on the ground floor. The upper part was completely ruined, which actually offered some protection.

One evening, two Guardsmen were lightly wounded by a mortar bomb. I treated their injuries and decided to take them to the Medical Officer in the Crypt for extra first aid supplies. It was a well-known rule in Casino never to go out alone; although I didn't, I ended up going back by myself after the Medical Officer evacuated my two casualties.

I hadn't gone far when the Germans opened fire with machine guns and mortars. Hearing the whistling of a mortar coming down, I dove for the ground just as it exploded nearby. I felt the blast and must have blacked out for a moment. When I came to, I quickly checked myself to make sure I was in one piece before trying to get back to House Mary.

Just then, I heard some voices nearby. A group was approaching; they sounded German. I jumped to my feet, dashed to House Mary, and informed the CSM about the German patrol moving toward the Crypt. The Signallers quickly alerted HQ, and a search party was organized. I ended up leading the way back to where I had heard the voices.

Imagine my surprise when those "Germans" turned out to be a group of Welsh Guards making their way out of Casino! After a mortar explosion right next to me, I was on high alert and couldn't easily tell the difference between German voices and Welsh ones! Of course, I was ribbed for that later: "Heard any Germans tonight, Corp?" Thankfully, No. 2 Company HQ returned to the Crypt the next day!

The days leading up to the push for Casino were filled with confusion. We knew the attack was imminent; two journalists showed up at our HQ, eager for interviews with the Germans holed up in the two hotels across from us, "The Hotel De Roses" and "The Hotel Continental." Our Platoon received extra ammunition, loudspeakers were set up, and everything was ready—but we still had no idea what our specific role would be.

When our signallers shouted the start of the bombardment, it was immense. We could also hear messages coming over the radio from the infantry and tanks. Our Platoons began firing into the German positions to give the impression that the attack was coming from our side. Meanwhile, the entire line from Casino to the coast was on the move. The Germans expected a push from Casino, which caught them off guard; however, they still fought back fiercely, causing many casualties on both sides.

Once again, we were fortunate. The two journalists, despite our warnings to stay put, decided to grab their equipment and dash across

"No Man's Land." There was a loud explosion, and tragically, two dead journalists were the result.

After the explosion, we finally emerged from our cellars and saw Casino in daylight for the first time. But as soon as we heard the loud bang, we quickly scurried back inside, fearing it was the start of a German bombardment. Only after learning about the reporters did we venture out again. I remember looking up at The Abbey, and what a joyous sight it was to see the Polish flag flying over the ruins! Just as we were breathing a sigh of relief at not being sent to chase the Germans out of Casino, we received orders to clean our cellars, gather our supplies and blankets, and prepare to move within the hour.

By May 28th, 1944, we learned the Germans were slowing our advance along Route 6 and had fortified their defenses in a town called Arce, which sat on three hills: Monte Grande, Monte Piccolo, and Monte Providero. Monte Grande was our objective. However, we had no idea what the terrain would be like since no prior inspections had been carried out—our maps only showed the three mountains ahead.

As we approached our start line, our guns opened fire, and the Germans quickly replied. We were moving up with our rifles at the ready when one Guardsman stumbled and accidentally fired his rifle, hitting another in the hand. I attended to him, and when the CSM came over to check if I needed help, I told him I should take the wounded man to the field dressing station to grab more bandages. The CSM said I had 30 minutes before we advanced.

I took the wounded man back to the dressing station, got additional supplies, and started my way back to the line. I hadn't gone far when I heard mortar shells coming down close by, so I hurried. Just as I sensed a mortar drop, I dove down to the ground. There was a deafening bang, and the blast knocked me out momentarily.

When I came to, I was hit by the smell of smoke and the ringing in my ears. I stood up, trying to walk, but my left foot felt numb. I couldn't see well, so I had to rely on touch. When I felt around, I discovered my boot's heel was missing and I could feel blood. Just then, a jeep drove by, and I shouted for help. Two artillerymen lifted me into the jeep, and I was taken to a clearing station. I don't remember much until I woke up in a hospital near Caserta.

The battle for Monte Grande had been brutal! Number 2 Company suffered over sixty casualties and failed to take their objective. The following day, they attempted it again, but by then, the Germans had retreated, allowing the Coldstream and Welsh Guards to achieve their goals.

My parents received a telegram stating I was missing, presumed dead—this was simply because the men in the jeep had taken me to the wrong clearing station. It wasn't until two months later that I was found by the Battalion. I was quite comfortable in the hospital, enjoying a nice bed, good food, and attentive nursing staff. In the bed opposite me lay a wounded German soldier from the 1st Parachute Regiment. He had been in Casino but was injured before the battle of Monte Grande.

At 7:00 a.m. on June 6th, we heard the radio announce the landings in France. The German soldier couldn't believe it; we all cheered like mad, but he insisted it was just propaganda. Even weeks later, when I left the hospital, he still wouldn't believe us. It was as difficult for us to accept Dunkirk and the surrender of Singapore!

I was discharged from the hospital at the end of June after about six weeks. Since I had trouble walking and couldn't stamp my foot, I was downgraded for three months. I ended up in a Guards Reserves camp south of Caserta, where I was put in charge of the Regimental Aid Post (RAP). The camp was well organized, and the RSM was a Coldstream Guard. I was pleased to receive a third stripe, which meant I could enjoy the Sergeants' Mess.

However, the camp also had a cage where British soldiers who had deserted and been arrested awaited their court martial in Caserta. I had plenty of problems with these men; they had nothing to lose and would take huge risks to escape. One prisoner, in particular, sneaked out every night to be with his girlfriend who worked in the Officers' Mess! He was caught trying to break back in, especially since two other prisoners had escaped the night before and were found twenty miles away. The camp guards were on high alert, waiting for them when our friend showed up, crawling back under the wire. Unfortunately, his girlfriend lost her job, One morning, I was with the Duty Officer inspecting the tents and mess rooms, including the pens where the more violent prisoners were kept. One deserter, awaiting trial, had already attacked his guards. The officer insisted on inspecting the pen; as he entered, the prisoner lunged at him with an open razor, slashing downward. Luckily, the razor hit the wired top of the pen, which deflected the blade, sparing the Officer's face. Together with one of the guards, I managed to grab the prisoner and disarm him. He was handcuffed at the wrists and ankles and sent to the main prison in Naples.

At that time, there were thousands of deserters in Southern Italy, each a mixed bag of characters. It was hard to pin down which nationality had the most, but since the British and American Armies had the largest presence, the number of deserters was relatively low. The Italian Mafia was a real headache, stealing loads of supplies from Army warehouses!

As my foot improved, I asked to rejoin my unit and was transferred to the Guards Holding Battalion. Reinforcements for various infantry battalions were in high demand, so soldiers who had been wounded and fully recovered could be assigned to any regiment. This didn't sit well with many British soldiers, especially the Senior NCOs and regulars. Luckily, the Guards had the privilege of their own Holding Battalion to supply reinforcements as needed, although replacements were still short in supply. Many of our reinforcements came from the RAF Regiment, and they fitted in really well.

While waiting to join my Battalion, I kept my third stripe and acted as a Sergeant. For a time, a group of Guardsmen worked with the Military Police in Naples, which was struggling with a gang led by a dwarf known as "El Gormo." He used Army deserters to raid Army depots and steal vehicles. The black market was rampant, and the Palace in Naples served as a sort of NAAFI for every soldier—even those working for El Gormo. Occasionally, the Military Police would raid the Palace, rounding up several deserters. Our job was to surround the Palace and prevent anyone from escaping. I believe El Gormo was eventually shot during a raid on his hideout in Rome.

By the time I was back with my Battalion in Spoleto, it had been decided that the 5th Battalion would return to the UK and disband. Most of the 5th Battalion would replace older soldiers in the 3rd Battalion, many of whom had served through France, Africa, and Italy. I had held back my return for six months, thinking I would reunite with my friends in No. 2 Company. Unfortunately, when I finally arrived, they had all returned to England. The unit felt different, and I felt isolated. There was so much happening, leaving little time to sulk. Those who went back to the UK could become reserves for the Battalions in France (the 1st, 2nd, and 4th). Although this didn't ultimately happen, it was a possibility at the time.

The 3rd Battalion returned to the 6th Armoured Division, but most of the Guardsmen were new, and a full training programme was implemented. We left Spoleto and billeted in Fermo to complete our training. Fortunately, Fermo had escaped the worst of the war, and we received a warm welcome from the locals. We trained alongside tanks and did our best to impress the residents. Several romances bloomed, but I doubt any survived our stay.

By April 1945, the fighting had shifted hundreds of miles north of Fermo. The Gothic Line was broken, and the New Zealanders, Poles, Indians, and the 8th Army were making significant progress without us. We began to think our presence at the front wasn't needed—but that was just wishful thinking. The 6th Armoured Division was being held back, waiting for a decisive move.

The breakthrough finally came at The Argenta Gap, opening up the plains beyond—ideal for an armoured division. On April 18th, we started our journey through Ravenna and onto Ferrara. After nearly two weeks of waiting, we were finally on the move again. Once more, we could hear the guns and explosions. Many newcomers in the Battalion had never been in action before! The breakthrough put the Germans in disarray; for once, they had misjudged our intentions, and the

Americans broke through on our left flank. The German Army had been ousted!

We spent hours crawling on our stomachs as enemy outposts showered us with machine gun fire; anyone who dared lift their head was likely to get hit. I was busy moving from one wounded soldier to another, surprisingly without a single fatality to report. One young Lieutenant, newly assigned to the Company, thought crawling on his stomach was beneath him. As he sat up, a bullet zipped between his legs and damaged his wedding gift. All he could do was moan about how his young wife would react to his injury. There was no way I could put a dressing on that! Sometimes I wonder how he managed to survive—I can't remember his name.

The Battalion raced to keep up with our tanks. One village, San Bartolomeo, was defended, and we were tasked with clearing it. Luckily, just before our attack, the RAF launched a good "stonk" on the village, causing the enemy to vanish and leaving us with only a few prisoners to take. Hearing the cries of the local population was disheartening; normally, we would have helped them dig out, but our orders were clear: "Push on. Do not let the enemy regroup." With the Germans eager to cross the River Po, it was crucial that we reached the bridge over yet another canal, so we couldn't stop to help civilians.

When we reached the bridge, we found it had been destroyed. Fortunately, we could cross the debris, but it was slow. The Germans kept up a steady fire from their heavy machine guns, and we scrambled across under their bullets. Our orders were to "press on" and penetrate the German line as far as possible; we never imagined we could get cut off.

Fortunately, the tanks and armoured cars of the Derbyshire Yeomanry charged through and captured hundreds of prisoners. We then moved to a nearby village where we paused, with the River Po just ahead. The 3rd Battalion Grenadier Guards were set to make the initial crossing. Along the way, we had found two beautiful horses that were too valuable to be left behind, so I took it upon myself to sell them to a farmer for 120,000 Lira. It took ages to count that money! After we divided it up, I managed to send a cheque for £40 to my mother—though she never received it. By the time I found out, I had already been demobbed!

Crossing the Po felt like a nightmare to all of us; the Germans had spread leaflets portraying the river as a massive watery grave for anyone who attempted to cross. No. 4 Company and No. 1 Company were the first to make their way across at about 1:00 a.m. on April 25th. Every second, we expected the heavens to rain down thousands of shells on us. We had braced ourselves for losing about half the Battalion, yet surprisingly, we only had one casualty—I only heard a single rifle shot. By chance, we landed on an unguarded stretch of the Po. Later, some prisoners revealed that the German relief Battalion had failed to arrive, which is a classic situation in the Army—sometimes the left hand doesn't know what the right hand is doing! It was oddly reassuring to know the Germans also faced such confusion.

The Battalion quickly dashed on to surround Gaiba, with No. 4 Company leading the way while my Company (No. 2) encountered no resistance. We followed No. 4 Company and took positions on the outskirts. Although we had caught the Germans off guard, they quickly regrouped and formed a force large enough to counterattack since we only had three Companies across the river. Fortunately, No. 4 Company captured a senior German NCO who was carrying a message from HQ to organize an attack. Because of his capture, the Germans decided not to attack and instead withdrew.

By the next morning, we had enough units across the river to advance further, aiming to cut off the German retreat before they reached the mountains (The Alps). The Americans had also breached the German defensive line near Verona and Milan. German Command had lost control, leading to white flags being raised all around us, although there were still a few groups wanting to fight. In one incident, No. 4 Company was about to cross a bridge when it was blown up. Fortunately, there were no casualties; they scrambled across the canal, commandeered bicycles, and rushed on to Adige, crossing another bridge and stopping just short of Lemdinara, which was defended.

Little did we know, while our war was coming to a close, our problems with the Italian partisans and the Yugoslavs were just beginning. As mentioned earlier, the Americans had broken through the German defences at Verona and were racing to cut off all access points to the Alps, encircling the Germans who were still trying to reach the safety of the mountains. Although we were all on the same side, our rapid advance caused some confusion, leaving a few red faces.

Back at Army HQ, the breakthrough by the 6th Armoured Division, including the 1st Guards Brigade, had thrown their plans into disarray. Most of the follow-up supplies—rations, fuel, bridges—ended up in the wrong places. Thankfully, this didn't hinder our advance since the German Commander had lost control. The 8th Army (British) moved quickly and soon faced challenges in supplying the forward troops. Bridges over the River Po and Adige needed to be rebuilt, and our lack of backup troops allowed the Yugoslavs to take over while the Italian partisans ran rampant.

The Battalion spent most of our time collecting prisoners, believing the battle for Italy was over. All it seemed to require was a phone call from Brigade HQ to activate us again, sending us towards the towns of Udine and Cividale. The Yugoslavs regarded that area as their territory and had already claimed much of the food and occupied the main buildings. Their soldiers were rough and undisciplined, while the Italians saw us as their protectors.

There were some tense moments, like when our Drum & Fife band played "Beat Retreat" in the town squares. Luckily, our discipline and behaviour helped to keep the peace, and meetings between the Chiefs of Staff and Tito eventually smoothed things over.

D-Day Dodgers

Lady Astor, Tory MP christened the troops in Italy the "D-Day Dogders". The following song, sung to the tune of "Lily Marlene" was written in reply.

> *We're the D-Day Dodgers out in Italy*
> *Always on the vino, always on the spree.*
> *Eighth Army scroungers and their tanks*
> *We live in Rome - among the Yanks.*
> *We are the D-Day Dodgers, over here in Italy.*
>
> *We landed at Salerno, a holiday with pay,*
> *Jerry brought the band down to cheer us on our way*
> *Showed us the sights and gave us tea,*
> *We all sang songs, the beer was free.*
> *We are the D-Day Dodgers, way out in Italy.*
>
> *The Volturno and Casino were taken in our stride*
> *(A Canadian version goes "The Moro and Ortona were taken in our stride.)*
> *We didn't have to fight there. We just went for the ride.*
> *Anzio and Sangro were all forlorn.*
> *We did not do a thing from dusk to dawn.*
> *For we are the D-Day Dodgers, over here in Italy.*
>
> *On our way to Florence we had a lovely time.*
> *We ran a bus to Rimini right through the Gothic Line.*
> *On to Bologna we did go.*
> *Then we went bathing in the Po.*
> *For we are the D-Day Dodgers, over here in Italy.*

Lady Astor forgot that we had had four D-Days prior to the one that is mostly remembered; Algeria, Sicily, Salerno and Anzio. In Italy alone, we suffered over 310,000 casualties, killed, wounded or missing. Major battles included Salerno, Casino, Anzio and The Gothic Line, including the River Po. Many served four and a half years without home leave. Yes, Lady Astor, we are the D-Day Dodgers over here in Italy.

Lottie and Ivy with me at Buckingham Palace receiving DCM in 1947

Back Home

We finally returned to England on 29th July 1945 and were sent to Hawick in Scotland. We were meant to have two weeks of leave, but first, we had to undergo an inspection by our Colonel-in-Chief, HRH Princess Elizabeth (now Queen Elizabeth II). While on leave, I was enjoying a party thrown in my honour by my Aunt Rya when the news broke that the Japanese had surrendered, meaning my service in the Army was coming to an end!

132

After reporting back to Hawick, I learned that the Battalion was heading to Palestine. All the men who had signed up for the duration left Hawick and moved to a Nissen hut camp near Slough. It was there that I spotted a poster offering courses for demobilised members of the Armed Forces in subjects like English, Maths, Science, and Foreign Languages. The course lasted six weeks, and after six years in the Army, I realised I could use a bit of re-education, so I signed up—and I was the only one!

I was sent to Edinburgh to a college just outside Peebles. I found myself as the only soldier, surrounded by officers from the Army, Navy, and Air Force, both men and women. My first Maths lesson was about Logarithms, and while I had studied them back in school, the lecture was way beyond my grasp. The instructor, a Major, paused after a few minutes and asked, "Do you all understand so far?" I stood up and admitted, "I haven't understood anything you've said, Sir." I sat back down, and the tutor looked around the room. At first, no one moved, and I thought I was going to be dismissed. But then hands started to raise, one after another, until nearly half the class had put their hands up. The tutor decided to go back to the beginning and explained Logarithms and how to use them.

At the end of the six-week course, we had an exam on the three subjects we'd chosen. I didn't do brilliantly, but thankfully I wasn't the worst! After that, we had a meeting with the Senior Officer, and I shared my thoughts on the course, saying it was excellent and that another six weeks would really prepare me for civilian life. I didn't expect to get the extra six weeks, but to my surprise, I was called back to see the Senior Officer and actually received the additional time!

During our leisure periods, I participated in Scottish Dancing, and during the final session, we had a special visitor—none other than General Montgomery (Monty) himself. He noticed my African Star and Italian Star, so he came over to chat with me. He asked about my experiences in North Africa and Italy (including Casino) and my DCM. We also discussed how I was enjoying the educational course, and I praised it, suggesting that every serviceman should attend a similar course. Everyone seemed happy with my response.

When I returned to camp, I realised I had missed my demobilisation. But soon after, I received my orders and set off for Manchester, where I was to be demobbed in a warehouse in Oldham.

After the War

I first met Ivy after the war when I found it hard to settle down. I wore my demob suit, and it seemed like every man I came across was wearing the same outfit. I needed to decide on a job; I was interested in joining the Police Force, but it felt too much like the Army, and I would have to move away from Birkenhead. Instead, I chose to return to Lewis's until I figured out my next move. I went back to the furniture department, under my old manager, Joe Coughlan. He had become a Major after spending four years in India and Burma with the Liverpool Scottish Regiment.

While on demob leave, I met Ivy Jones, who was also on leave after spending four years in the WAAF. We first crossed paths at a dance in Hulme Hall, Port Sunlight, and our romance blossomed in April 1946. By December of that year, it was time for me to introduce Ivy to my family. I had spent the last seven Christmas Days in the Army, and I thought this one would be special.

The houses on Dacre Street were terraced and had once been considered quite nice, with three bedrooms, a kitchen, a dining room, and a parlour—though no bathroom; the toilet was down the yard, which was freezing in winter!

By then, eight of us would be sitting down for Christmas dinner: Mam, Dad, Frank, Raymond, Gerald, Alan, Ivy, and me. I really should have discussed bringing Ivy with my mother more thoroughly. I had mentioned it, but it must not have registered. You can imagine the panic that ensued when I reminded Mam that Ivy would be coming along, as I went to meet her at Central Station. I felt a bit like a man about to be hanged!

Seating eight people at our dining table wasn't easy. A large fireplace with an oven on one side and a hob on the other made it cramped.

Sitting with your back to the fire felt like being in the depths of Hell, so Gerald and Alan ended up there.

Mam always cooked a fantastic Christmas dinner. She insisted on doing it her way, and nobody dared to interfere. There was no parade of the turkey into the dining room for carving; Mam carved and served it all herself. Each plate was heaped with all the trimmings, and they were brought two at a time, meaning your dinner could be cold by the time everyone was served. Gerald got the last plate, and just as Mam handed it to him, there was a loud crack and a smash—he was left holding a piece of the plate while the rest and its contents lay scattered on the floor. Our cat, Buller, wasted no time and jumped right in to eat the turkey!

Without a word, Mam took all the plates back to the kitchen, and Raymond quickly cleared up the mess. By taking a bit from each plate, a new plate was prepared, and we all finally received our meals, enjoying the dinner together. I was worried about Ivy's reaction, but she said she had enjoyed every moment and thought my mother was exceptional. In fact, Ivy and Mam became good friends!

Christmas at 64 Dacre Street was always special. I think it was the decorations and the trips to either Lewis's or the Cooperative store to meet Father Christmas and receive a Grotto present that made it magical—those presents were saved until Christmas Day, of course! Our stockings would be hung over the fireplace, and on Christmas morning, we'd rush downstairs to find them filled with nuts, an apple, an orange, chocolate pennies, a shiny new penny, and maybe a game like Ludo or Snakes and Ladders. The dining room would be decorated with coloured paper and balloons; it was the one time of year when everything was bright and cheerful.

As we grew older, we started attending Midnight Mass, and after Mass, we would go to Nanna Byrne's at No. 3 Robert Street. Her tiny two-up, two-down house became quite cramped as our family grew, especially when some relatives popped in as well. Nanna always treated everyone to a fried butty—bread dipped in bacon fat and fried until crisp. I can almost taste it now—wonderful!

Since then, I've tried to keep the spirit of Christmas alive. At our current home in Sale every Christmas morning, we invite friends and our children over to our house. Now, we even have our grandchildren joining us, and we hope to continue this tradition for many more years. Father Christmas has been visiting us every year since 1962, and I hope he'll keep coming for many years to come.

In July 1948, Ivy and I got married. I was working at Lewis's as a trainee manager, and Ivy was working in Bon Marché in Liverpool as a sales assistant, selling ladies' separates, blouses, skirts, and more.

Left to Right, Lil (Ivy's sister in Law), Bill Forrester (Best Man), Lottie (my Mam), James Byrne (my Dad) Joice Aspey (age 5) Me, Ivy, Ivy's mum, Ivy's Dad John Robert Jones, Alan (age 4) Margaret (Ivy's sister) Gerald (age 6)

At that time, Birkenhead was facing a housing crisis. The Germans had heavily bombed the town, making it nearly impossible to find available housing. Ivy's friend, Mary Aspey, had just taken over a semi-detached house on Thistleton Avenue. With Mary and her husband having two children, they kindly allowed us to move in, and we felt extremely lucky.

During this period, furniture, bedding, and carpets could only be bought with coupons or vouchers, plus a hefty amount of cash. A friend of Ivy's had emigrated to Australia, and after her mother passed away, she left behind all her household furniture. Ivy was given the first choice of that lovely furniture, far better than the utility pieces available at the time. We had to furnish a bedroom, a living room, and a shared kitchen—quite a challenge for newlyweds!

We enjoyed a comfortable life in that house for two years until Mary informed us she was pregnant with her third child, which meant we had to move out. Around that same time, Ivy's mother wasn't well, and her father worked long hours, sometimes seven days a week. With all of Ivy's siblings married and moved out, we decided to move in with her parents. It was the perfect arrangement for all of us, and we enjoyed being together.

Then, Ivy found out she was pregnant. At this point, I was the Assistant Manager in the food department at Lewis's, and we knew it was time to think about getting a place of our own. Ivy went into hospital, but tragically, the baby—a girl—died during childbirth. It was a bitter disappointment, especially since I was raised alongside eight brothers.

We continued to stay with Ivy's parents, where Ivy helped care for her mum. Two years later, Ivy was pregnant again, and we were excited, especially since her parents were looking forward to the birth of our child. Unfortunately, just weeks before our son, Keith, was born, Mrs Jones passed away and never got to see her grandchild.

Finding new accommodations was tough. I joined a group planning to buy land to build our own houses. We needed tradesmen—bricklayers, plumbers, electricians, and so on. We had found a suitable plot and had decent tradesmen lined up, but getting planning permission became a major headache. Just when I was about to pull out of the scheme, I was promoted to Staff Manager in our Leeds store. My predecessor, Pat Gamble, had returned from holiday but collapsed and died just before coming back to work. I was appointed to take his place, a role he had filled with great respect, and it was a challenging job for me.

Ivy and I moved to Leeds in January 1957, with Keith almost five by then. We bought our first house at Number 26 The Quarry in Alwoodley—a lovely place that was only about five years old. Keith adjusted well to his new school, and we soon settled into life in Leeds. Shortly after settling in, Ivy found out she was pregnant again, and our second son, John, was born the following June.

John's arrival wasn't easy; he had a significant swelling on one side of his face that took a long time to go down. We worried it might be permanent. To make things worse, Ivy contracted pneumonia and was ill for quite a while.

My promotion to Staff Manager was a big deal. I spent six years in Leeds, where the store was thriving, employing nearly 1,000 staff with a well-balanced mix. During my time there, I worked with four different General Managers, which turned out to be beneficial for me. The General Manager relied on the Staff Manager to provide insights about the staff and their abilities. I developed a good rapport with two of my GMs, Bill Bayley and Henry Cotton, which was quite fortunate. Having several General Managers helped boost my confidence and my standing with the Board of Directors.

Overall, our time in Leeds, which lasted nearly six years, was very pleasant. Our neighbours were simply the best!

Moving to Manchester

In August 1962, I was promoted to Manchester to work as the staff manager, overseeing 3,000 employees and 200 demonstrators. The Manchester branch of Lewis's was the largest store in England outside of London.

I served on various committees in Manchester, mainly as Chairman of the Chamber of Trade. During this time, the city was undergoing significant changes, including the construction of the Arndale Centre, the largest shopping centre in Britain at the time. As a result, I was in touch with the City Council almost every day. The city centre was one massive building site; the public stayed away, and trade was suffering tremendously. The Council was eager to raise the business rate. Some of their suggested increases were outrageous! Very few of the larger stores were making a profit, but because these organisations had an overall profit, the left-wing members of the Council argued that they could afford it. Fortunately, the leader of the City Council owned a shop run by his wife, so he understood our concerns.

I organised fashion shows in the store, with the profits going to the Lady Mayoress's favourite charity. This led to Ivy and me being invited to lovely events in the Lord Mayor's parlour and various functions. Eventually, when Father Christmas arrived at his Grotto in Lewis's store and made a stop at the Town Hall on his way, it resulted in Christmas fairy lights decorating the entire city centre. Many other cities contacted me for information—I even had a lovely visit to Belfast to speak with local retailers.

When we moved to Manchester, our younger son John was five years old. He and Keith attended Brooklands Junior School in Sale, and both enjoyed their time there. Keith later went on to Sale Grammar School, while John won a scholarship to Manchester Grammar School. They both excelled in their studies.

In 1979, I was promoted to Assistant General Manager of our Liverpool store; it felt like the clock had gone full circle! On my first morning, the General Manager was away, leaving me on my own. I arrived at the store by 8:30 a.m., walking around and chatting with staff to get to know their names and roles. Then, the fire alarm went off. The flashing lights indicated the location of the fire, so I dashed down to the ground floor perfume department. A new door had recently been installed, and the extractor fan overheated, triggering the sprinkler—water was everywhere! Luckily, several staff members and porters were around with sweeping brushes, quickly clearing the water out the door while a barricade of sawdust prevented it from spreading.

By the time the Fire Brigade arrived, everything was under control, and the Fire Chief praised our initiative. I returned to the third floor and used the TANOY to congratulate the staff on their quick actions and inform them of the Fire Chief's approval. When I stepped onto the third floor, the staff gathered around, clapping and cheering. It turned out nobody had ever thanked them before! As I walked around, I received applause on my very first day—what luck!

Not long after that, we held a "Staff Day." The Staff Council took over the Senior Manager's roles, swapping duties throughout the store. I started as the "Staff Lift Driver" and later took on porter duties, while the General Manager worked in

In the basement at Lewis's, Jack Byrne, assistant manager, brushes up the day's rubbish in January 1978

the Food Department. Our Publicity Manager met several newspaper reporters at the Adelphi Hotel and told them about our Staff Day. Since there was no exciting news that day, every daily newspaper featured photographs and stories from our day—a stroke of luck! Remarkably, our store saw a significant influx of customers that week.

I retired from Lewis's in 1983. By then, I had become a part-time member of the Industrial Tribunals and a part-time member of the VAT Tribunals, which kept me quite busy. I had to be careful not to earn too much because of the higher rate of income tax. I travelled around the country to sit on various tribunals, and it was fascinating work. I wouldn't have been able to do all that travelling if I were still working full-time. This career lasted until 1990 when I turned 70.

Passports Please

Ivy and I were thrilled when our son, John, told us he'd be spending 4 weeks in Paris, with a French family, all organised by Manchester Grammar School. In exchange, 2 French boys would be coming to stay with us in Sale a few weeks later. Since John needed an individual passport, his name was removed from our family passport, but I had nothing to do with the process—it was all handled by his school.

The following year, I won a French frame tent in the Lewis's Tombola. So we decided that the whole family—Ivy, Keith, John, and I—would go on a camping holiday in France, focusing around Royan. The lead-up to the holiday was quite hectic, with planning the route, checking the tent, and gathering all the equipment. We planned to drive down to Southampton and take the night boat to Cherbourg, then motor down at our leisure.

We arrived in Southampton in plenty of time and joined the queue to board the boat. When the Customs Officer checked our passports, he looked into the car and said, "Sir, you have three names on your passport and four people in your car." That's when it hit me—John's personal passport was back at home in Sale, a whopping 300 miles away! What on earth was I going to do?

I pulled out of the line of cars, and silence filled the vehicle. I spotted a Customs Office, went inside, and spoke to a young man, but he wasn't much help. I could apply for a 24-hour passport, but the photo machine was out of order. As I walked back to my car, I noticed the officer who had stopped me at the barrier getting into his car and driving away. I decided to take a chance and try to board the ship.

I joined the queue again; it was now past 10:00 a.m., and our boat was set to sail at 10:30. I handed my passport and boarding pass to the attendant, and to my amazement, he waved me through—what luck!

Once on board, we found our cabin, and the boys quickly set off to explore the ship and meet other children. Most of the other passengers were aware of our predicament, and several offered suggestions, but nothing appealed to me. However, I appreciated their good wishes. My next hurdle was getting through the Police at Cherbourg. A couple of passengers even promised to help me out.

When I approached the Gendarme, the two chaps in the car ahead pressed their horn and held it down, prompting several other cars to do the same. To my surprise, I was waved through! I didn't stop the car for at least 20 miles afterward.

Eventually, we stopped in a small village, and I was glad to stretch my legs and relax. I had decided to leave the passport issue until my return, but that was easier said than done. First, I wrote John's name back in my passport, smudged the page with oil, and hid the passport under the bonnet to keep it safe.

As I left the village, I turned down a narrow road, suddenly realising it was a one-way street and I was going the wrong way. To make matters worse, I spotted a Police car further down the road, parked and watching. I slammed on the brakes, put the car in reverse, and executed a slick maneuver to turn around. Unfortunately, in my haste, I knocked over the one-way street sign! I didn't stop to check my car or the sign—I just had to get as far away as possible.

I had to show my passport at every campsite, but that wasn't an issue. I couldn't risk staying in a hotel, as you had to leave your passport at the desk, and the Police examined them every night. I found myself eager for the end of this holiday.

On the way back to Cherbourg, I noticed the driver in the car behind me flashing his headlights. I thought he wanted to overtake, but there was nowhere for him to pass, so I continued on. He kept flashing, so I pulled over onto the grass verge, and the driver stopped, calling out, "Balloona, Balloona!" I checked my tyres, which seemed alright to me, but the Frenchman pointed to the inside of my wheel. There was a massive bulge just waiting to burst! I thanked him as he drove off.

First things first, I unloaded the car and jacked it up to change the wheel. However, after loosening the nuts, I discovered that the jack had sunk into the grass. After a few choice words, I moved the car onto solid ground, changed the wheel, reloaded the car, and we set off for Cherbourg.

We hadn't travelled far when a car sped past us erratically with luggage on a roof rack. Suddenly, I saw a large suitcase bounce towards me. I swerved to avoid it, narrowly missing the first case, only to have a second one fly by, bursting open in the process. The driver seemed oblivious, probably thinking my flashing lights were a sign of annoyance. I have no idea how far he drove before realising his luggage had been left behind. I turned off after a bit, having seen the car behind stop to collect the suitcases. My thoughts were now focused on my conversation with the British Consul in Cherbourg.

We arrived in Cherbourg at 3:00 p.m., and I had no trouble finding the Consul's office. I sat in the car rehearsing what I would say. When I finally stood at the Consul's door, I took a deep breath, rang the bell, and waited. It felt like an eternity before the door opened; I found it odd that the Consul's office would be closed. A woman dressed in what resembled maid's attire answered. Her English was poor, and my French was even worse, but I eventually understood that the Consul was closed for the day; everyone was on holiday until Monday. What good would Monday do me?

It became clear I would have to risk returning to the ship. I joined the queue and boarded without any issues. Once aboard, the real challenge was obtaining the landing tickets the next morning.

At 6:30 a.m., the first call went out for people with British passports to collect their landing tickets from the Purser's Office. The announcement repeated every ten minutes as I waited for the final call. When I approached the Purser's Office, I explained that I was late because I couldn't find my passport. Before I could say much more, the Officer asked, "How many tickets do you need?" I stammered, "Four: two adults and two children." I was handed the tickets and rushed back to my anxious family.

Once off the ship, I raced to get out of Southampton and back on the road home to Sale in Cheshire. And so ended a holiday I shall never forget.

However, one problem still loomed—my forged passport. I considered various options, but many were quickly dismissed. I lay awake at night coming up with excuses that just wouldn't work. The easiest way out seemed to be to damage the passport and return it to the main office in Liverpool. I decided to put it in the washing machine for a good wash, rinse, and spin cycle. When the passport emerged, it was completely unreadable!

I then received a new passport, and for the first time in months, I could finally relax and start planning my next holiday.

Father Christmas at Lewis's

As the Assistant Staff Manager at Lewis's in Liverpool, one of my responsibilities was to recruit the staff for the Christmas Grotto. This included three women, two fairies, two men to help carry things and manage the queues, and three men to play Father Christmas.

The arrival of Father Christmas ready to open the grotto

The lead Father Christmas was crucial; he needed to have a good appearance, charisma, and authority, as the Grotto was a major event during the Christmas season. It could make or break the store's trading results for the entire year. The top Father Christmas had to be at least 5 feet 8 inches tall, have a kind face, and know how to engage with children.

I encountered some challenges finding the right person—perhaps I was trying too hard. I considered asking the Theatre Group for help, but they were quite expensive! Just as I was about to admit defeat, I found myself interviewing a distinguished-looking gentleman. I couldn't believe my ears when he expressed interest in becoming Father Christmas. He explained that he had recently retired after earning his pension, giving him the freedom to pursue new opportunities. To my delight, he mentioned that he had been the Mayor of his town, which I verified while he filled out his application. I thought, "What luck!"

The arrival of Father Christmas went off without a hitch, and the first couple of weeks unfolded according to plan; everyone was pleased. Then, one morning, the General Manager called me into his office. It happened to be coffee time, so I thought I was in for a friendly chat. However, the moment I walked in, I realised I had been invited for anything but coffee. The GM thrust a letter into my hand and said sternly, "Explain that!"

The letter was from an irate mother whose child had been eagerly looking forward to meeting Father Christmas in the Grotto. Initially, everything went well, but then the mother felt Father Christmas's hand on her knee as he spoke to her son. His words took a suggestive turn when he remarked about Mummy giving him a big kiss. He pulled her closer and kissed her while his hand slipped under her skirt. In shock, she grabbed her child and ran out of the store as fast as she could. She later realised she should have reported the incident to the manager.

I was at a loss for words. I knew the man would deny any wrongdoing, and without evidence, it would be her word against his. I remembered the mother mentioning that he smelled of alcohol; that was our lead. With the help of our Store Detective, we plotted the best way to catch him in the act of drinking.

We waited nearly two weeks until he left the store one lunchtime. We enlisted the help of an attractive lady, an ex-policewoman with a young child. She agreed to assist us. We even set up a camera to record the behaviour of our Father Christmas.

Everything went according to plan. He followed the same routine as the woman had described in her letter. We promptly had him arrested and charged before he could gather his thoughts. As usual, the case dragged on, and I was transferred to Leeds before it went to court. The man was found guilty and sentenced to six months in prison. The story made the front page of the Liverpool Echo, and thank goodness the article didn't disclose which store it had happened in!

This incident taught me the importance of ensuring that I always obtained good references, both written and verbal, for any new staff. Between 1956 and 1979, I was involved in organizing the arrival of Father Christmas and his Grotto at Lewis's stores in Liverpool, Leeds, and Manchester. In my opinion, Liverpool always provided the most exciting Grotto experience—it felt very real to the children. After all, it was the store where I'd seen my very first Father Christmas back in 1928 when I received a German helmet as my Grotto gift.

The Lewis's Bomb

Monday, 27th January 1975, is a day I will never forget. Our new General Manager, Mr. R. Greenhalgh, was introduced to us at 11:00 a.m. By 3:00 p.m., he called a meeting with all the senior managers. As we settled in, the signal lights began to flash, indicating a bomb warning. During this time, we were getting bomb alerts almost daily.

Since I was responsible for security, I excused myself and informed the General Manager that I would report back as soon as possible. I knew the managers in their departments would carry out the search procedures. I rushed down to the control point, which was at the staff entrance. As I arrived, a Police Inspector appeared, confirming that the bomb warning was official. Just as I lifted the phone to update the General Manager, there was a tremendous explosion.

The fire alarm light indicated an emergency in the basement, so the Inspector and I dashed down there. What I found was a disaster area— the lights had blown out, and moans and screams echoed in all directions. When the emergency lights flickered on, I saw wounded people lying everywhere, with staff and customers helping the injured while more assistance arrived. I quickly realised my role was at the control point, so I went back and directed the evacuation of the store.

The managers had executed their evacuation procedures efficiently. The ground floor was packed with customers making their way out. I was concerned that there might be a second bomb. By then, the control point was crowded with Police, Firefighters, and Press representatives. A quick chat with the Police Inspector ensured everything was running smoothly. I contacted the managers to confirm their staff roll calls. The Police cleared the streets, and ambulances whisked the wounded away to hospitals. Meanwhile, reporters and TV crews clamoured for interviews and tried to access the building.

Our staff gathered in Piccadilly Gardens. It was January, and at 4:00 p.m., I arranged with the Police to let a few staff members go back into the store to collect their coats from the cloakrooms. It was more complicated for those stationed on the top floors and in the sub-basements. Staff came out carrying ten or more coats belonging to their colleagues. The number of injured was at least 32, and tracking exactly how many had been hurt was tricky since several hospitals were used. Most injuries were minor, although one draughtsman lost an eye. Thankfully, nine of our staff were among the wounded, but none had serious injuries.

At home, the television was on, and in a newsflash, I appeared on screen recounting the incident. This was around 5:00 p.m., and I didn't make it home until about 8:00 p.m. The offices and shops in the area were incredibly supportive, taking care of most of our staff on that cold, fateful day.

We never discovered if the bombing was the work of the IRA; they denied responsibility, but "the password" was given to the Police. A letter from Castle Douglas in Kirkcudbrightshire, Scotland, arrived shortly after. I had been stationed there in 1941, and now, in 1975, an ex-girlfriend recognised me on television—once seen, never forgotten!

As far as I know, the person or group responsible for the bombing was never found. Interestingly, five more bomb explosions occurred the following day, all in the London area. It's possible that the Manchester bomb was a diversion to draw attention away from the South.

Security

In a large store, there are many pitfalls that can eat into profitability. To counter these losses, money is spent on security, which requires close cooperation between Departmental Managers and the Security Staff. In my day (1962-1983), the responsibility for liaising and managing the Security Staff lay with the Staff Manager.

Shoplifters employed various clever tactics. One I remember involved a fancy cardboard box placed atop a display of gloves. The base of the box was loose, allowing the shoplifter to lift it and pull goods inside. This method could be used for gloves, stockings, handkerchiefs, perfumes, and more. The shoplifter came across as cool, calm, and pleasant—but when she was caught, a search of her home revealed thousands of pounds worth of stolen goods. She had a stall at a market in Bury, and the items were traced back to many stores in and around Manchester and Liverpool.

Another tactic involved disguising a theft with a billowing skirt to hide stolen items tucked away beneath. There were so many methods that it was a constant challenge to keep up with the changes. The introduction of mobile cameras fitted on the ceiling was a significant breakthrough, although it was challenging to monitor all departments simultaneously. Still, it certainly helped reduce losses.

Staff pilferage was another major issue. We tried various methods to combat this, and with careful attention from the Manager and assistance from external sources, we could mitigate the problem. However, it was always lurking. Stealing cash from the till would put the whole department under suspicion, and once we identified a rogue employee, it was usually just a matter of time before we caught them. We had our share of surprises; in one case, the culprit turned out to be the wife of a very senior person on the City Council. The store policy was to prosecute every case, which sometimes created headaches for the Staff Manager.

Another issue arose when staff arranged for friends to act as customers, receiving goods for little or no money, pretending they had already paid. Managers had to stay vigilant about the various tricks staff used to obtain goods without paying.

One significant loss of goods occurred in the Liverpool Store. It was obvious the thefts were happening outside store hours. After investigating the evening cleaners and finding no evidence of theft, the store detective and I conducted an extensive investigation and deduced it had to be the night painters employed by an outside firm. We decided to keep our plan quiet and didn't even inform our superiors. We set up two television cameras to monitor the painters in the menswear department.

The first four nights yielded no evidence, leading us to think our suspicions might have been mistaken. However, on Friday night, everything fell into place. At the end of their shift, three painters were seen removing goods—ties, shirts, underwear, suits, and men's trousers—clearly gathering items to fulfil an order. As they left the store, they were made to unload their lorry, which contained their ladders, paints, brushes, and covers. When we opened the covers, there was the "loot," carefully packed away! This eventually led to the prosecution of over twenty individuals. The case took ages to reach court, but by that time, I had been transferred to our Leeds Store.

Pickpockets were always a problem too, and despite our repeated warnings to the public, many women believed, "It could never happen to me." However, the pickpockets knew exactly who to target. In some cases, customers would write to us anonymously, providing little information but expressing frustration that they would never shop with us again. Ironically, one of our female store detectives had her purse stolen. We were fairly certain we knew who the pickpocket was, but since we hadn't caught him in the act, there was nothing we could do. In the end, we did manage to catch him, but not while he was in Lewis's!

1988 Royal Garden Party Ivy and Myself waiting to be presented to HRH Queen Elizabeth 2nd. (Top Middle, arrowed)

Ex–Grenadier meets Queen

A RETIRED Grenadier Guard and Sale resident Jack Byrne has been presented to the Queen at a Buckingham Palace garden party.

Jack was one of 200 members of the Manchester branch of the Grenadier Guards Association, and one of about 5,000 people, who attended the party held to celebrate the 75th anniversary of the association.

Mr Byrne and his wife, Ivy, were presented to the Queen, who is the Colonel-in-Chief of the Grenadier Guards, and she asked them questions about themselves, their family and about their involvement with the regiment.

The event also gave Mr Byrne – who served in the Grenadier Guards for six -and -a- half years and was awarded the DCM for his services in Tunisia during the Second World War –the opportunity to meet a lot of former friends and collegues.

Said Mr Byrne : "Both myself and my wife had a fantastic day – it was out of this world".

RECOLLECTIONS

WIRRAL | *Wartime hero's cause for celebration*

A tale of bravery

- *Tending casualties under fire gained John a medal*

by Andrew Davies

It is always interesting to hear a story of exceptional bravery during wartime, but for one Wirral hero July will bring an event almost as significant as a golden wedding anniversary.

John Byrne, now 78, was awarded the Distinguished Conduct Medal for his outstanding gallantry while serving as a medical orderly in North Africa aged just 23.

John was a Lance Corporal in the Grenadier Guards serving in Tunisia during 1943. During an attack on the enemy stronghold of Altifiga Hill, near Bou Arada, the Guardsmen took heavy fire and many were wounded. The ground was rocky with almost sheer slopes and dotted with thick scrub, and John and his team of stretcher-bearers worked under incessant sniper fire.

At one stage, John and another bearer carried a Lance Sergeant to an aid post over terrain so difficult that it took them nine hours to travel two miles.

On the way they dressed and attended six other wounded men.

His citation reads: "According to all reports, the powers of stamina displayed by Lance Corporal Byrne were amazing. As a result of his work 30 casualties were tended under fire and successfully evacuated."

John is modest about his bravery. "Although I was awarded the medal, I was only part of a team. My friends Tommy Higginson and Wally Kershaw were alongside me all the time and, interestingly enough, they were also from Wirral."

The war, of course, brings happy stories too, and during a dance at Hulme Hall in Port Sunlight John met his future wife Ivy, then in the WAAF.

They married on July 3, 1948 in St Anne's Church, Rock Ferry and John returned to his job as a salesman at Lewis's.

John and Ivy now live in Sale, Cheshire where they are close to their two sons, Keith and John and their five grandchildren.

They are holding a huge party next month to celebrate their 50 years together.

LINES AREN'T AN OPTION

HAPPY ● John and Ivy on their wedding day

Sunday Afternoon Trip – December 1997

Ivy and I had planned to visit Chester that Sunday. It seemed like a great idea at the time, but after a night out with friends on Saturday, returning home after midnight, I didn't wake up until late Sunday morning. By the time we had breakfast, it was almost midday. Instead of Chester, we decided to take a drive through the beautiful Cheshire countryside, passing through Knutsford, Holmes Chapel, Congleton, Macclesfield, Alderley Edge, Wilmslow, and Ringway, before heading back home to Sale.

As we reached Macclesfield, I decided to take the A536. I had never driven on that road before; it wasn't fast but was busy enough, and I was enjoying the trip. I was leading a string of cars, but as I approached a right-hand bend and pulled to the left, I suddenly heard two loud bangs almost simultaneously. The steering wheel nearly jumped out of my hands, but I managed to keep the car steady. I could tell the car wasn't running properly, so I spotted a side road up ahead and turned into it, while the other cars continued on, likely having seen me struggling.

Once I pulled over, I inspected the car. There was no damage to the bodywork, but my rear tyre was flat. I couldn't see any other damage, so I considered calling for help, but there was no telephone nearby. I decided my best option was to change the tyre myself. It didn't seem too difficult, but I had never done it before. Imagine my panic when I couldn't find the jack or any tools! Where could they be? I realised I might have to call someone for help.

I saw a house with a car parked outside, so I walked over and rang the doorbell. A man about 40 answered, and I asked if I could use his phone to call for help. He inquired about my car troubles, and after I explained the situation, he came over to take a look. He then offered to change the wheel himself and disappeared for a moment, returning with a professional car jack and tools. I was amazed at how quickly he changed the wheel. He mentioned he owned a garage in Congleton—what luck! When I asked him how much he wanted for the help, he simply replied, "Happy Christmas," and before I could express my gratitude, he was gone. I didn't catch his name or address, but I planned to retrace my journey to send him a thank-you letter.

When I got home, I told my family and friends about my stroke of luck in getting help from that kind man who owned a garage. The next morning, I took my car to the local tyre service. I was told the repair would only take ten minutes, so I waited in the office. That's when I discovered the front tyre on the same side as the one that had been flat was also damaged. As a result, I had to spend an additional £47—not quite the luck I had hoped for! Whatever I had hit that Sunday afternoon must have been incredibly sharp!

Ladies Day – 4th June 1998

Today is Ladies Day in Neston, Wirral, an event that, as far as I know, is the only one of its kind still held in England. This colourful and enjoyable pageant is an annual tradition organised by the 250 Club, a ladies-only group that raises funds for charities. Established in 1814, this event is now 184 years old! On Ladies Day, children aged between 5 and 12 are allowed to walk in the parade, marking the culmination of a year of fundraising for various charities.

One longstanding tradition is for the ladies and children to dress in outfits reminiscent of Party Time in 1814, which means the dresses and hats are exceptionally attractive. The parade kicks off with at least 100 children leading the way, followed by a band—in this case, a very smart Pipe Band. After the band, over 100 ladies follow, all looking beautiful in their long dresses and bonnets. Each child and lady carries a large bouquet of flowers, tied to a decorated stick with long ribbons trailing behind. These bouquets are meant to symbolize a Maypole, a popular feature in 1814.

The procession makes its way into the Parish Church, where the service lasts about 30 minutes—just enough time for a cup of tea! Once the service is over, the procession heads to The Cross in the Town Centre, where we gather with priests, town dignitaries, the Mayor, and local councillors. Everyone joins in singing hymns and prayers, and then the band leads us to the British Legion Hall for refreshments.

Meanwhile, the Fairground is buzzing with activity, continuing throughout the day until 11:00 p.m. Neston Ladies Day is definitely not an event to miss! The only downside is that the day is never properly publicised; it seems to be a well-kept secret to ensure the occasion remains exclusive for local residents. Who can blame them for wanting to keep it special?

The Neston Female Friendly Society is also very active, dedicating their work to charity—not just for those in Neston but for all the needy, sick, and disabled individuals in the Wirral area. Ladies Day signifies the end of a year's work and the beginning of a new one.

Golden Wedding – 3rd July 1998

Friday, 3rd July 1998, marks exactly 50 years since Ivy and I tied the knot at St. Anne's RC Church in Rock Ferry. Back then, I was a Trainee Manager at Lewis's store in Liverpool, which was a large organisation consisting of seven department stores and several smaller ones, with Selfridges in London acting as the head office.

To celebrate our Golden Wedding, Keith and John insisted on throwing a party at the Cresta Hotel in Altrincham. They invited 80 of our friends, and it turned out to be a wonderful evening. Keith took charge of the event, and it was a huge success—especially the singing group, comprised mainly of members from the Gilbert and Sullivan Society, of which Ivy was a part. Six of my brothers were there, along with Ivy's sister, my best man Bill Forrester, and his sister.

The concert party wrapped up around 11:30 p.m., but the audience wasn't ready to let them go. Luckily, my brothers had a coach waiting, and the driver was running short on time. It was a lovely evening—well planned, and John did a fantastic job of circulating among the guests and introducing everyone. We were fortunate to have friends from all over England join us to celebrate our Golden Wedding.

I must mention my friend Willy Pullman, a Director at Lewis's and a keen photographer. He spent the entire evening capturing video recordings around the hall. He later gifted me an excellent video of the night, which isn't just a recording of the event; it tells the story of our 50 years of married life together, blending those memories with the highlights of the celebration. So, thank you, Willy!

Jim

My brother Jim was born eighteen months after me on 14th August 1921. He was as blonde as I was dark, lightweight while I was heavy, and gentle where I was rough—truly my opposite. But he was a Byrne, and like the rest of us, he was stubborn; it wasn't easy to get him to change his mind. During our childhood, we mostly kept out of each other's way. Jim had his friends, and I had mine. However, as part of the same gang, he accepted my role as the leader, and he was always loyal—not once did he let me down.

While I was Nanna Byrne's favourite, Jim was Nanna Kay's. Nanna Kay encouraged Jim to take lessons with Mr. Butler, the woodwork master at our school. He also practised on our piano. So, it made sense that Jim would be the one to organize any plays or concerts our gang put on. You might wonder why plays and concerts were part of our lives—quite simply, there was no radio, leisure centres, or organized play areas back then. Our entertainment was entirely self-created. Jim gathered a group of six to eight boys to form a concert party.

Just before the war, Jim joined the RAF as a regular, eager to be a wireless operator. When war was declared, he volunteered to be a rear gunner—why, I'll never know! Rear gunners didn't usually live long; however, Jim was posted to Rhodesia and stayed there for three years. He was demobbed around 1947. Soon after, he married. His wife, Doreen, was a lovely girl with auburn hair, a warm smile, and a strong will.

For a time, Jim worked as a salesman at Owen Owen in Clayton Square, Liverpool (as did my brother Tom). After a while, he felt there was no future for him there, so he moved to a furniture group called The Times. He was a good salesman and enjoyed his work until the last few years. Unfortunately, when the company was taken over, they lost their management skills, and loyalty wasn't valued. As Jim approached his 64th birthday, he learned that his shop in Grange Road, Birkenhead, was closing down. While his colleagues were informed about their futures, Jim wasn't, which worried him. His immediate manager was on holiday at the time, and the uncertainty of unemployment weighed heavily on him.

Jim had already suffered two previous heart attacks; while they hadn't been serious, they had damaged his heart. The stress of the shop closing and the lack of information about his future proved too much for him. On Thursday, 6th August 1985, he suffered another heart attack. Initially, he was seriously ill, but after three critical days, he pulled through. When Ivy and I visited him on 12th August, he was sitting up in a chair and seemed quite chatty. He mentioned that the danger had passed, though there was some fluid on his chest. Sadly, Jim's birthday was on 14th August, and he died in his sleep early that morning. We all thought he had survived the attack; how wrong we were! Just hours after Jim passed away, his daughter Wendy gave birth to a baby girl. "As the Lord giveth, so the Lord taketh away."

As strange as it may seem, we never discussed his wishes for burial or cremation. Being a good Catholic, Doreen assumed he would have preferred to be buried. We had a family grave, so it was decided Jim would be interred with our parents. On 19th August, we all attended the Requiem Mass at St. John's RC Church in Rock Ferry. Father Clarke led the service, the organist played, and the choir sang beautifully. The church was packed. I never realized how popular Jim was! My family alone comprised 40 people, and many neighbours, colleagues, old school friends, Scouts, and RAF members were there.

Father Clarke was exceptionally kind; his sympathetic manner touched us all, especially Doreen, Wendy, and Stephen. But Jim was gone. Of all my brothers, he was the kindest and most gentle. He always took the time to listen, help, and support those in need. We will miss him dearly. If there is a place called Heaven, I'm sure Jim is there, preparing a warm welcome for us all.

Tom

Tom was born on 29th October 1927, joining our family of four brothers: me (John), Jim, Frank, and Martin. His arrival felt automatic; there had always been a baby in the house, and this tradition continued with four more brothers: Raymond, Stephen, Gerald, and Allan.

As the eldest, it was often my responsibility to look after Tom. Whenever possible, I'd put him in a pram and take care of him for the rest of the day. My gang was all boys, and taking a pram around with a baby posed a bit of a challenge. Thankfully, some members of the gang had sisters who loved to push the pram around, allowing the boys to get on with the usual adventures.

Tom probably experienced our gang's antics better than I can recall his growing up. He would surely remember the time when the girls got caught raiding an orchard for pears and apples—though at that age, he was still young enough to be in the pram!

Tom handled his schooling without any fuss and attended St. Hugh's RC School when the war broke out. Due to the heavy bombing in the

Liverpool area, he was evacuated to a charming little village called Buckley, just over the border in Wales. It was a lovely place, not too far from Birkenhead.

Ivy's Story Ivy's words

It was a lovely autumn day with blue skies, the sun shining, and the air feeling clean and fresh. It wasn't the kind of day to stay inside listening to the radio, but there I was, along with my two friends, Mary and Nancy, my mother, and my brothers Harry and John. My father was at work. We listened to the Minister, Mr Chamberlain, as he declared, "We are therefore in a state of war with Germany." At just 17 years old, I didn't fully understand what that meant. We had been at war with Germany before and had beaten them. There had been plenty of talk about their build-up of planes and tanks, which they had used in Spain. We knew about them, and according to the rumours, they were professionals. Despite their might, we believed we could match them, even with weapons dating back to 1918!

My friends and I decided to take a walk through Bidston Pine Woods, over Bidston Hill, past the windmill, and along the top, where we overlooked the River Mersey and the Irish Sea. If Germany planned to send planes to bomb us, we thought we'd spot them and bring them down before they crossed the Channel. Still, it felt unsettling looking out over the sea, waiting to be bombed. Eventually, we realised it was lunchtime. War or no war, Sunday lunch was sacred, so we hurried home and temporarily forgot about the war and Mr. Chamberlain.

National Service was already in full swing, and any young man aged twenty could be called up. We only knew of one boy who had been called up, but several others in the TA had been put on alert. In fact, within weeks, they were off to war. My friend Mary decided to get married to Les, who was about to be called up. Les joined the Cheshire Regiment and saw action in France at Dunkirk. Thankfully, he made it through the war, and he and Mary are now proud grandparents.

The bombing of our town, Birkenhead, was dreadful. One night in March 1941, a landmine exploded right in front of our house. Fortunately, we were all in our air-raid shelter at the time. When we finally came out, our house was gone; I was devastated. My mother told me to go to work at the local Co-op in the grocery department, as people would need food. I was relieved to see the shop still standing, even with its shattered windows. The manager, Mr Baker, was busy sweeping away the rubble and broken glass. He told me to give every customer one ration of tea, sugar, butter, and bacon, along with anything else depending on the family's needs. Most customers had lost everything and didn't even have the means to cook or make a cup of tea. The shop quickly became a meeting place.

As a result of the raid, my family was split up. I ended up living with my friend Nancy and her parents until I joined the WAAF.

On a previous air raid, I had been on my way to a dance when the sirens sounded, so we took cover. When the "all clear" sounded, we carried on to the dance. Although there was a sense of foreboding, we had accepted that "what will be, will be." If our number was up, we figured there was nothing we could do to prevent it; we had grown somewhat fatalistic. However, as we approached the dance hall, the sirens sounded again, and we took shelter as bombs dropped. One hit the dance hall, killing several people. We ran back to our homes as bombs continued to fall all over the town. Eventually, I got home to find my family distraught—our dog, Gyp, had been killed. The devastation was immense; Birkenhead and the Liverpool Docks were ablaze. The bus and tram depot and the gasometer had been hit, all caught in the firestorm. It felt impossible that anyone could survive that inferno. Yet, when dawn broke, townspeople emerged from the rubble, staring in horror at the ruins of their homes. Some began searching through the debris for their belongings, trying to salvage what they could. It was a heartbreaking sight.

I served four years in the WAAF, mostly stationed in Blackpool. My duties varied, but I spent much of my time in the stores, issuing equipment to airmen going overseas. I was demobbed in 1946, and during my demob leave, I met my future husband, Jack, who was also on leave. Jack had served in the Grenadier Guards in North Africa and Italy, earning a DCM for bravery while carrying wounded men under fire.

Now, I have two sons, Keith and John, and I fervently pray they will never experience a day like September 3rd, 1939, or all the events that followed the announcement of WAR

John's closing notes:

My dad was a remarkable man, very straightforward, but determined. He was a tough father but softened with time and when he retired, and we introduced his grandchildren Matthew, Nicola and Louise to him and later Keith and Sara's boys Jack and Tom he was very kind and enjoyed his time with them.

Lewis's was big part of Jack's life and both Keith and myself were able to work Saturdays and Holidays. Keith worked in Lewis's record shop and this helped him establish himself a very capable DJ for parties and weddings and he was good at it. Keith moved into the Insurance industry permanently and was training to be an underwriter (which he never really enjoyed) when he went on a Club 1830 holiday in Ibiza he didn't come home but stayed there to become a Rep. As you can imagine dad was furious saying no future in it. Thanks Keith! Left me to suffer dad's wrath. Keith progressed with Club 1830 to become Sales and Marketing Manager. He was able to stand in front of huge crowds at Club 1830 reunions and get everyone going. He met and married Sarah in Surrey, and moved back up north to work for Cresta Holidays which he loved.

Jack took Ivy to Tunisia to visit the graves of fallen comrades, unfortunately Ivy fell and broke her knee, from which never recovered and was unable to walk without aid. Mum also developed Parkinson's and dad was diagnosed with Dementia. Slowly they both grew old and increasingly required more and more support which Keith and I organised with exceptional help from Sharon and Sarah.

Over time conversations became harder. I mention this because unfortunately Keith became ill with pancreatic cancer, we agreed to not tell mum and dad, which was probably a good idea at the time. But at some point though, I knew I would have to tell them he was not here. As it became clear Keith needed to go to hospital for palliative care I started the process over three days, "Remember last week I said Keith was unwell ……..' Keith's funeral was incredible, the large church was packed and there were people standing outside, he was a hugely popular man and had 100's of friends and colleagues in the travel industry and he is still greatly missed. Mum and Dad sat at the front of the church and I remember dad saying "whose funeral is it?", it was such very sad time.

Jack passed a few months later and the Brigade of Guards sent two Guardsman to stand at the Church doors and as guard of honour, respect.

Ivy followed Jack a couple of months later.

Jacks Eulogy delivered by John

Hello thank you all for coming, I know Jack will appreciate it

As you all know (and Father Butterworth has mentioned) mum's condition dictates that she can't be here. She is quite comfortable in her own space singing her Gilbert and Sullivan songs and doesn't really understand what is going on around her.

To be honest, what I am about to say about Jack, he has probably already told you himself, as Dad wasn't backwards in coming forwards.

Those amongst you who have sat in Sale Golf Club or Brooklands Sports Club over the years will not be surprised by the things I am about to say

You knew exactly where you were with Jack,
You knew what he thought and why

and he often told you what he thought **you** should think **too**.
His point of view was never in doubt,

And he was always certain
even when he was completely wrong **HE** was certain.

I can say these things, because these were part of his defining characteristics

He was honest, ………………… painfully at times
Hard working, …………………… always
Loyal, to all his friends and especially to mum who he loved dearly
He was always Supportive to friends and family

Mostly though …………. he was a good friend to all of us

Alf Worsley summed it up for me last week on the phone when he said

"Jack was one of the those people you would **always** want on your side"

Dad spent many many hours after retirement drafting his memoirs by hand and I intend to read some short extracts today

He started writing in May 1981 and I quote the first 2 lines

"The first day of spring March 21st is a good day to be born and 1920 is also good year as it makes it easy to remember you age".

Jack was the eldest of 9 boys, and he was born on 21st March 1920 to Charlotte and James Byrne. 64 Dacre St Birkenhead

Jim, Frank, Martin, Stephen, Tom, Raymond, Gerald and Alan followed dad not necessarily in that order
Spring 1925 Jack started school   St Lawrence's Roman Catholic,
He says
"I enjoyed the freedom at school, at home there was so little room, at school I had a seat and my own desk !!!   I was introduced to the cane at the age of 7"

His journal goes on to talk about his spare time on Saturdays at the age of 10 or so, dad used to borrow the milk cart from Coughills dairy and go to the gas works on Hind St and load up with 6 bags of coke at 3 pennies each which he would sell at 6pence a sack. 100% mark-up not bad and early signs of retailing skills

When dad left school he applied to various companies for work
Lever Bothers
The Leather Works
Woodsons
And Lewis's department store, his and our world would have been very different had he been successful in one of these other roles

Actually none of these had any vacancies at that time so Dad's first job was working for Reg Johnson in Birkenhead market initially delivering meat on a push bike. Often at weekends proudly taking a beef joint and sausages home to Nana Byrne

Lewis's eventually offered dad a job **12 months later ,** which he accepted, he started in the bakery at the age of 16 (1936)

Lewis's became a huge part of his life and a great part of my family's life

Most things dad set his mind to he achieved

For instance he joined the Cubs at the age of 8 and by the age of 16 he was a King Scout the highest possible position for a scout.

And as a king scout he was selected to attend the Coronation of George 6th London and Lewis's paid his expenses

Sunday September 3rd 1939, the day war was declared, dad was at the chalet at Dodd's farm which he and a group of friends rented, Jack McKinley, Harold Brooks, Bill Yates, Fred Sessford, Bill Forrester and Jack - war was declared and the talk was of joining up.

Dad Joined the 3rd Battalion Grenadier Guards in Nov 1939 having lied about his age as many did he trained at Caterham and was first posted to Windsor

This had, **I am sure it's the same for all of his generation**, a massive influence on the rest of my dads life. He was very proud to be a Grenadier Guard and he had endless stories of his adventures and escapades.

I will not dwell on this period simply read this extract from his citation

**"On Thursday 4 February 1943 L/cpl Byrne and his 3 stretcher bearers worked without a break for over 24 hrs,
the conditions in which they laboured were appalling, difficult terrain and heavy mortar and machine gun fire and deliberate sniping.
These did not deter L/Cpl Byrne and his bearers…….. As a result some 30 casualties were tended under fire and successfully evacuated"**

For his selfless courage in North Africa Dad was awarded the Distinguished Conduct Medal.
What is less known is that dad wrote to the his local paper about Wally Kershaw and Tommy Higinson two of his bearers asking for their bravery to be acknowledged too.

John Anthony Byrne DCM

Adams with an A and Byrne with a B meant that Vic Adams and Jack Byrne were often rostered for duties together and became lifelong friends along with Eric Tyson, Bill Yates and many others. I remember Vic and Eric very well and I still have and use a fishing rod Vic gave me.

In April 1946 Dad was on his demob leave when he met Mum - Ivy Catherine Jones at a dance. Mum was also on demob leave after 4 years in the WAAF

As my uncle Alan says - she was a vision of beauty

Dad's journal says
Christmas 1946 It was time for me to introduce Ivy to my family and Dacre st
At that time there would be eight for Christmas dinner Mam, Dad, Frank, Raymond, Alan Ivy, and me. I should have discussed my idea of bringing Ivy more fully with my mother, you can imagine the panic when me and Ivy turned up and no place was set for either of us. The plates went back into the kitchen to be shared out
Ivy and mam became great friends

Dad married my mother on 3rd July 1948 at St Annes Church Rock Ferry and Bill Forester was his best man.

A place to live was provided by Mary Aspey one of mums life long friends (and who I spoke to last week) They stayed with Mary for the first two years of their marriage. They then moved in with mums parents in 10 Richardson Road.

A certain sparkle was lit in July 1954 when Keith was born

At the same time Dad was promoted to Assistant Staff Manager in Liverpool by Fred Richardson the then Staff Manager who was a good friend and mentor to dad.

A year later dad was promoted again, this time to Staff Manager and they moved to Leeds 1955 and I was born in 1957, so I am the only Byrne from Yorkshire
We moved to Manchester in July 1962 again with dads job

19 Westmorland Road
and for me the most typical example of Jack Byrne behaviour -- he thought if I am to get to know my neighbours we need to ask them round for drink – so he chose Christmas day lunchtime to do it.

Unbelievably successful, some years we have seen as many as 40 people turn up

for 39 years people came -- even people who had moved away, still turned up for a quick drink with friends in the middle of their own busy Xmas day

With the arrival of the grandchildren - Father Xmas also turned up with prezzies for the kids

Rubbish prezzies but it was a fantastic tradition

it was only 2001 when it finished and Father Xmas at last got a rest on Xmas day

Xmas day never quite felt the same once that had stopped

well done Dad   and Mum who also cooked a Xmas dinner whilst chaos ensued

I am not sure when dad took up golf but it was another large part of his life, dad played mostly with Derek Andrews and Don Bowden every Sunday and often straight after work in summer

Mum and dad celebrated their 50th wedding anniversary in 1998 which Keith organised and many of you were there - it was a great celebration and we were pleased we did it.

The early loss of Keith was a great strain on both mum and dad and much of their sparkle went with him, they were heart broken.

So the last couple of years have been quite sad

I gain great strength from Sharon and my kids who are all very supportive, and from Sarah and the boys who are busy creating life after Keith in Surrey.

But we also get great support from Mary and the amazing band of carers who have looked after mum and dad so well,

they do a fantastic job and they do it from the heart

but you can only give your heart if you love the people you care for

and we ALL loved Jack   even though we probably wouldn't tell him

Printed in Great Britain
by Amazon